Devils Gate Wy

~BMT

SAINTS AT DEVIL'S GATE

SAINTS AT DEVIL'S GATE

LANDSCAPES ALONG THE MORMON TRAIL

LAURA ALLRED HURTADO

BRYON C. ANDREASEN

FEATURING THE ARTWORK OF

JOHN BURTON, JOSH CLARE, AND BRYAN MARK TAYLOR

THE CHURCH
HISTORIAN'S
PRESS

CHURCH HISTORY DEPARTMENT EXECUTIVES

Steven E. Snow

J. Devn Cornish

Reid L. Neilson

DIRECTOR, CHURCH HISTORY MUSEUM

Alan D. Johnson

DIRECTOR OF PUBLICATIONS

Matthew J. Grow

EDITORIAL MANAGER

R. Eric Smith

EDITORIAL STAFF

Hillary Olsen Errante

R. Eric Smith

DESIGN

Wayne Pullman

THE CHURCH HISTORIAN'S PRESS is an imprint of the Church History Department
of The Church of Jesus Christ of Latter-day Saints, Salt Lake City, Utah,
and a trademark of Intellectual Reserve, Inc.

www.churchhistorianspress.org

Front cover (composite image): Detail from (left to right)
John Burton, *Wonders of His Love* (Red Butte, Wyoming, 2016);
Josh Clare, *Praise Ye His Name* (Casper, Wyoming, 2016);
and Bryan Mark Taylor, *This Too Shall Pass* (Rocky Ridge, Wyoming, 2015).

Back cover: Josh Clare, *Rock of Ages* (Devil's Gate, Wyoming, 2014)

Inside front cover: Bryan Mark Taylor, Untitled, sketch (Devil's Gate, Wyoming, 2013)
ii: Josh Clare, *Dawn Color*, paint study (Osceola, Iowa, 2016)
iv: John Burton, *Last Light on Scotts Bluff*, paint study (Scotts Bluff, Nebraska, 2014)
vii: John Burton, *Winter at Chimney Rock*, paint study (Chimney Rock, Nebraska, 2014)
viii: Josh Clare, Untitled, paint study (Winter Quarters, Nebraska, 2015)
xi: Bryan Mark Taylor, Untitled, sketch (Mormon Ferry, Wyoming, 2013)
xii: Josh Clare, *Scotts Bluff*, sketch (Scotts Bluff, Nebraska, 2012)

Monochrome detail:
xiv: Josh Clare, *Light of Life* (Fremont County, Wyoming, 2016)
10: John Burton, *A Prayer for Shelter* (Devil's Backbone and Rock Avenue, Wyoming, 2016)
15 & 16: John Burton, *Golden Light* (Between Big Mountain and Little Mountain, Utah, 2015)
122: Josh Clare, *Does the Journey Seem Long?* (Near Richardson's Point, Iowa, 2015)
134: Bryan Mark Taylor, *Flat and Wide* (Platte River, Nebraska, 2016)

ISBN: 978-0-692-78585-0
Library of Congress Control Number: 2016955283

Printed and bound by Brigham Young University Press, Provo, Utah.
10 9 8 7 6 5 4 3 2 1

CONTENTS

Acknowledgments x

Editors' Note xii

Foreword xiii
by Jean Stern

"More Wonderful Than Beautiful": Painting the 1
Land along the Mormon Trail
by Laura Allred Hurtado

"Oh How I Wish Mine Were a Painter's Pencil or Poet's Pen": 11
Pioneer Reflections on the Landscape of the Mormon Trail
by Bryon C. Andreasen

Saints at Devil's Gate: Exhibition 16

Interview with Artists 123
John Burton, Josh Clare, and Bryan Mark Taylor
by Laura Allred Hurtado

Notes 135

Further Reading 141

Contributor Biographies 142

ACKNOWLEDGMENTS

This exhibition catalog is made possible through the assistance and support of many individuals and institutions. We give special thanks to the executives and advisers of the Church History Department of The Church of Jesus Christ of Latter-day Saints for sponsoring the project and to the management and staff of the Church History Museum, who provided a venue, support, and expertise for the exhibition.

The project of painting the Mormon Trail was initiated in 2011 by artists John Burton, Josh Clare, and Bryan Mark Taylor. Bob Brown gave access and context to the property surrounding Mount Pisgah, Iowa, and artist Grant Redden provided navigational support in Wyoming. We thank Deborah and Don Groesser for their hospitality in Omaha, Rick Forschino for photography support, Lincoln Miller and California Archival Framing for framing the works, Gary and Alice Middlemiss for financial support of the project, and Robert Martinez for his enthusiasm. We extend special thanks to Jean and Linda Stern for their great contribution to the arts and unending support of plein air painting and acknowledge with appreciation Robert and Louise Burton, David and Jayne Clare, and Mark and Laurel Taylor for their support of the project. We express our deepest thanks to Katherina Burton, Cambree Clare, Haley Taylor, and the Burton, Clare, and Taylor children for their unwavering support and sacrifice and for dealing beautifully with painting trips.

The bulk of the research was conducted at the Church History Library, Salt Lake City. Several other libraries and repositories also provided critical materials and assistance: Special Collections, J. Willard Marriott Library, University of Utah, Salt Lake City; Pioneer Memorial Museum, International Society Daughters of Utah Pioneers, Salt Lake City; Utah State Historical Society, Salt Lake City; and L. Tom Perry Special Collections, Harold B. Lee Library, Brigham Young University, Provo, Utah. We gratefully acknowledge Carol Cornwall Madsen, whose book *Journey to Zion: Voices from the Mormon Trail* provided much of the framework for this project, and Wallace Stegner, whose foundational work *The Gathering of Zion: The Story of the Mormon Trail* captured the spirit of the Mormon pioneers in narrative form.

We acknowledge with appreciation the contributions of many individuals from the Publications and Library Divisions of the Church History Department. We express gratitude to Shannon Kelly, Rachel Osborne, and Kathryn Burnside for checking sources and locating hard-to-find documents, to Nicole Fernley and Elizabeth Miles for assisting with intellectual property matters, and to Riley M. Lorimer for consulting on a variety of issues. Thanks are also due to the staff of the church's Publishing Services Department, particularly Maurianne Baker and Don Miles, who assisted with the editorial efforts, and Kellene Adams, Kelsi Walbeck, Deborah Bradford, and Stacie Heaps, who checked sources and verified quoted material. Steve Rogers supported us as a project manager; Nikaela Aitken assisted with printing arrangements; and Andrew Schmidt provided technological support. Marc Lunt of the church's Information and Communication Systems Department also provided technological support.

We extend special thanks to Thomas Hurtado and Glen Nelson, who reviewed early drafts and offered important feedback. We are also indebted to Mike Landon and Amanda Beardsley for providing valuable comments.

We express thanks to Jason D. Loscher and his associates in the Preservation Division, Church History Department, for scanning and photographing many of the images in this volume. Thanks also go to Ben Ellis Godfrey and Debra Xavier, Audience Needs Division, for their assistance with promotional efforts. We thank Brigham Young University Press for expertly printing and binding the volume. Ben Bean and Doug Maxwell were our helpful liaisons there.

We wish to thank the entire exhibition team. In particular, we thank Stacie Lusk for her insight and willingness to brainstorm ideas, and Anna Graff and Kelsie Tomlinson, who helped organize sketches. We also thank Nancy Anderson, Craig Rohde, James Ito, Mike Weber, Carrie Snow, Maryanne Andrus, Ray Halls, Jared Sano, Annette Burdette, Riley Lewis, and Kevin Nielson, as well as Jeremy Jacobsen, Greg Green, Benjamin Roberts, and team for their help in the exhibition construction. Thanks are extended to Ron Anderson for guiding the exhibition team on the Mormon Trail and to Chad Orton for his expertise on early Mormon Trail maps.

Finally, we wish to thank the pioneers, whose great faith and strength we celebrate and honor in this catalog.

EDITORS' NOTE

Documentation in this book comes from original sources to the extent possible and practical. In quotations from manuscript sources, the editors have silently standardized some spelling, capitalization, and punctuation to aid readability. Occasionally the editors added words to quotations to enhance clarity; such additions are enclosed in brackets. Biblical quotations are from the King James Version.

Most labels identifying the locations depicted in the artists' paintings use modern place names. Much work was done to pair the excerpts from pioneer journals with the general location represented in each painting; this was accomplished successfully in all but a few cases. In such cases, paintings were paired with quotations that generally addressed the trail experience rather than commenting on a specific location.

FOREWORD

Beginning in 2011, landscape painters John Burton, Josh Clare, and Bryan Mark Taylor decided to paint along the Mormon Trail, a route used from 1846 to 1868 by thousands of Mormons, many of whom were fleeing religious persecution. A good part of this historic trail follows the same route as the Oregon Trail and the California Trail, which were used by thousands of emigrants as they made their way west, but the aim of the Mormon Trail was to lead an oppressed people into uncharted territory, to a safe haven. Over the following months and in different seasons, together or individually, Burton, Clare, and Taylor continued to paint the trail until they had documented the prominent features of the route. The project to paint the Mormon Trail became both an artistic pursuit and a personal journey for the artists.

Like Burton, Clare, and Taylor, in 1853 the English artist and Mormon convert Frederick Hawkins Piercy (1830–1891) produced a series of illustrations that were published as engravings and woodcuts in the book *Route from Liverpool to Great Salt Lake Valley.* The book was intended to facilitate immigration of English Mormons to Salt Lake City. Years later, several of the Piercy images were combined with additional images by the noted American landscape painter Thomas Moran (1837–1926), who made the journey along the Mormon Trail in 1873. This pamphlet, titled A *Portfolio of Mormon Trail Engravings,* was published in 1874.

The exhibition *Saints at Devil's Gate: Landscapes along the Mormon Trail* features a series of beautiful oil paintings by John Burton, Josh Clare, and Bryan Mark Taylor, three award-winning landscape painters. These artists are noted for their remarkable ability to paint beautiful and elegant works, filled with natural light and brilliant color. Their graceful and sensitive views of the Mormon Trail appeal to all viewers, those who seek meaning and enlightenment in the historical background of the trail as well as those who seek beauty in art and nature. This memorable exhibition will have a lasting effect on all who view it.

Jean Stern
Executive Director
The Irvine Museum

"MORE WONDERFUL THAN BEAUTIFUL":

Painting the Land along the Mormon Trail

Laura Allred Hurtado

I first met the artist Josh Clare at a gallery opening in downtown Salt Lake City in September 2013. I responded immediately to the small collection of local landscape paintings then on display; they were tonal, with quick brushstrokes and rich colors that included sharp contrasts of light and dark. Some images had a beautiful sort of messiness to them, and then in other works was a sense of polished modeling in the rocks and trees that visually represented a location without belaboring it so much that it felt mechanically reproduced. That I liked the style was an understatement; however, as the art curator for the Church History Museum, I felt that the subject matter perhaps had little to do with the scope of the museum's collection. They were, I told myself, *just* landscapes.

My reticence changed when Clare emailed me with excitement weeks later to share images and descriptions of a project he was working on with John Burton and Bryan Mark Taylor, artists whose paintings were equally strong although stylistically different. Their project was called *Saints at Devil's Gate,* and it consisted of work by all three painters

capturing the Mormon Trail, the 1,300-mile route from Nauvoo, Illinois, to Salt Lake City, Utah, that mid-nineteenth-century pioneers traveled on their migration west.[1] The artists' intention was to pair their paintings with excerpts from historical trail journals by Mormon immigrants.[2] The exhibition at that point was largely conceptual; although a few of the paintings and preparatory sketches were years into development, little research—in terms of diving deeply into historical writing—had been done.

Yet, from the perspective of a curator, this project was potentially rich, a strong concept that fit our unique institutional mission, which blends history with art in ways that are at times precarious and tricky. Additionally, we knew as curators that the Mormon pioneer story would be missing from the museum after our reopening in September 2015. In curating the permanent exhibit *The Heavens Are Opened,* we decided to tell the story of the origins of our faith from the very beginning of the spiritual awakening that occurred in the first half of the nineteenth century in America and to end with a hint of the 1846 exodus out of Nauvoo. This

Detail of Douglas Fryer's mural *Nauvoo Temple,* installed in 2015 in the Church History Museum exhibition *The Heavens Are Opened.*

decision allowed us space to explore details of the church's founding that are often lost in a quick overview. But such a focus translated to the exhibition lacking any kind of serious reference to the revered Mormon pioneers, and we felt the gap even before we reopened. Beyond this practical consideration, what I saw in the project was an important reflection on viewing sites laden with history. Further, the artists' work explored nine-teenth-century modes of thought regarding the landscape as picturesque and sublime in ways that often mirrored the sentiments of Mormon pioneers as they crossed the plains.

For the three artists behind *Saints at Devil's Gate,* the project became more than creating paintings for an exhibition. It was also spiritual, a mix of professional practice and religious tribute. As they described the project, words such as *devotion, consecration,* and *conversion* often emerged. For Burton, a recent convert, there was a longing to bear witness to the land that was rooted in both his new testimony and the near-mythical stories of his Mormon ancestors. The original idea was Burton's, born out of a sense of a spiritual calling, as he described it.

The idea, of course, is not original. In 1853, British convert and artist Frederick Piercy took to the Mormon Trail with the intent of documenting noteworthy sites to illustrate the book *Route from Liverpool to Great Salt Lake Valley,* a type of illustrated handbook for British converts, an idea he conceived together with Samuel Richards, who was then president of the British Mission. Drawing and painting as he traveled, Piercy began in Liverpool, crossed the Atlantic, took a steamboat up the Mississippi River from New Or-leans, and stopped in Nauvoo and Carthage to pay homage to significant sites in Mormon history before completing

the journey west to Salt Lake City. Piercy also did portraits on his trip and, like Burton, Clare, and Taylor, had use of a camera (a camera lucida, to be specific) to document the various locations along the way.[3] What remains of Piercy's project is largely known through engravings and woodcuts made for publication, and the concept was primarily didactic. The end goal was to create a type of primitive Google Maps for potential immigrants. Piercy said, without exaggeration, that the sketches would "possess undying interest for tens of thousands."[4]

As it was for Piercy, it was import-ant to me to organize the paint-ings in a way that mapped them geographically, thereby creating an experience for the viewer that mirrors a journey.[5] But to map (and fix) the Mormon Trail now is partly a construction. In reality, there were many different trails, especially at the beginning of the westward trek in Illinois and the eastern parts of Iowa. So the viewing experience implies a type of linearity that didn't completely exist, even for those who followed Piercy's carefully laid-out guide.

Etching of Council Bluffs, Iowa, and a Mormon pioneer wagon train, from Frederick Piercy's book *Route from Liverpool to Great Salt Lake Valley,* 1855.

Additionally, while there are signposts that demarcate the official Mormon Pioneer Historic Trail (managed by the U.S. National Park Service), and while large sections still feel untouched, cities such as Casper, Omaha, Jeffrey City, Osceola, and Macedonia didn't exist as settlements at the time of the early Mormon pioneer migration. The artists' dream of returning to and documenting the historic path was, therefore, an imagined and inexact cartography; map-making, while posturing objectivity, is always a subjective process.[6] Both this project and Piercy's share an idealization of the trail, showcasing the highlights and removing the mundane and the unwanted vistas—civilization for Burton, Clare, and Taylor, and the dangerous for Piercy.

THE GETTYSBURG EFFECT

As with Piercy's project, the premise of the exhibition is direct enough, but the scope of it continues to yield meaning to me as a curator and to the museum staff. For example, the exhibition carries the symbolism of a land laden with history. For Piercy the migration was novel, but for Burton, Clare, and Taylor, who are all from the West, the landscape was familiar. It had come to signify a large portion of their (and our) religious legacy, and they looked at the land with what art historian David Morgan calls a "sacred gaze." Defining this sacred gaze as "the manner in which a way of seeing invests an image, a viewer, or an act of viewing with spiritual significance," Morgan adds that the gaze includes "the visual network that constitutes a social act of looking." This visual network consists of—but is not limited to—the artist, the audience, the subject viewed, the context of viewing, and the rules that exist between the viewer, the object, and the subject.[7] For Burton, Clare, and Taylor, spiritual significance was imbued in the land and in the act of painting, and the entire scope of the project as a visual network was, for them, sacred.

John Burton, *Exodus,* detail.

In John Burton's *Exodus,* craggy, uneven rocks fill the foreground (page 19). The Mississippi River is a warm, dusky blue, mostly calm, with waves lapping quietly on the far right. Stylistically, Burton's brushstrokes are loose, and paint is applied thickly. The feeling is impressionistic, capturing a fleeting moment of light that is just about to change, to move, to darken. The wide-angle composition shows Iowa as seen from the end of Nauvoo's Parley Street, the place where the earliest of pioneers would cross the near-frozen river beginning in February 1846 in the midst of anti-Mormon rhetoric, rumors of attack and harm, arson, and assaults.[8] The title *Exodus* frames the Mormon migration within biblical language (setting their struggle on par with that of the Israelites) and makes specific reference to that first wave of refugees, Brigham Young's so-called Camp of Israel, which involved three thousand Latter-day Saints evacuating midwinter instead of waiting for the planned departure in spring.[9]

In the painting, any reference to modern life in Nauvoo, which stands behind the picture plane, has been carefully cropped. The twilight sky imparts a sense of peace in the placid river. But the oncoming darkness also creates a foreboding feeling of loss and uncertainty. The road ahead is rocky, the trail rough, which hints again at the historicity of the site and acts as a metaphor for the finality of the distance between the earliest Mormon refugees and their former homes in Nauvoo. The first journal accounts are from those whose lives were in peril, whose homes were left behind, and whose conditions were abject and destitute; their three-wave evacuation would leave their utopic dreams of Nauvoo behind them. The painting's view, then, is one of nostalgia, looking away from a home that no longer exists, a home that is, as novelist Salman Rushdie describes, "imaginary."[10] Such careful cropping leaves the city as a ghost that exists only in the memory of how it was abandoned in 1846. To look back is to turn into a pillar of salt. Such visual exclusions can be read as largely symbolic: the absence of modern-day Nauvoo in the painting positions it as the homeland that cannot be returned to, that no longer exists.

And yet, many of the sites depicted in *Saints at Devil's Gate* have changed very little, if at all, since the pioneers' experiences with them 170 years ago. Landmarks such as Ayres Natural Bridge,[11] Rock Avenue, and Scotts Bluff would still be recognizable to the pioneers today. Independence Rock still holds memories within its granite, names of thousands of immigrants who passed through carved graffiti-like into stone.[12] It is difficult to view these locations through

This photograph captures the well-groomed landscape of modern-day Gettysburg, Pennsylvania, no longer the site of a bloody civil war.

our eyes without the stories of what happened there years ago echoing in the landscape, howling in the wind—the dust swirling with the atoms of kindred dead buried along the trail. Like the empty, grassy fields of Gettysburg, cleared of the bodies of fallen Civil War soldiers and long distanced from the smoke of cannon and rifle fire, the meaning of the landscapes of *Saints at Devil's Gate*

springs more from what happened there than from what can actually be seen in the landscape today, and the works of art are largely conduits of devotion.[13]

For Burton, Clare, and Taylor, the concept of pairing pioneer journals with their paintings allowed them to construct a singular persona that could stand for the whole of the pioneer experience. Like memorials where a fragment of a building or a single worn shoe stands as proxy for the trauma of a particularly horrific event or a symbol of genocide, these stories made the pioneer legacy personal, evocative, and accessible for the artists.[14] For example, Hosea Stout's loss of his wife and children shortly after the Iowa exodus was meaningful to Clare not only because of the gravity of Stout's loss but also because Clare's wife, Cambree, gave birth to their daughter Emily while he was working on the exhibition.[15] Burton's conversion in 2006 was, in part, sparked by his reading stories of the pioneers, specifically of his ancestor Robert Taylor Burton, whose legacy of faith inspired the artist to read the Book of Mormon. Looking for "nuance and a more rounded view of the Mormon story," Taylor read Wallace Stegner's *The Gathering of Zion: The Story of the Mormon Trail*.[16]

Additionally, all of the artists felt a deep personal connection to Martin's Cove and Devil's Gate. Their ancestors' lives—Robert Taylor Burton, Noah Brimhall (Clare), and John Watkins (Taylor)—converged as part of those dramatic and well-recorded scenes of terrible desperation. Watkins was a member of the Martin handcart company, and Brimhall and Burton were rescuers.[17] For the artists, such sites transcended neutral locations of geological interest or simply beautiful landscapes and were endowed with the memory of those who traversed there, made personal through the blood of ancestry.[18]

In a conversation with me about the Willie and Martin handcart companies, Taylor referenced sections of Wallace Stegner from memory and spoke of the meekness of those who, like his ancestor Watkins, suffered. Said Stegner,

> Perhaps their suffering seems less dramatic because the handcart pioneers bore it meekly, praising God, instead of fighting for life with the ferocity of animals and eating their dead to keep their own life beating, as both the Frémont and Donner parties did. And assuredly the handcart pilgrims were less hardy, less skilled, less well equipped to be pioneers. But if courage and endurance make a story, if human kindness and helpfulness and brotherly love in the midst of raw horror are worth recording, this half-forgotten episode of the Mormon migration is one of the great tales of the West and of America.[19]

The text consulted by curator and artist alike, Wallace Stegner's seminal pioneer history, *The Gathering of Zion: The Story of the Mormon Trail*, first edition, 1964. Marriott Special Collections, University of Utah.

With the minds of the artists filled with images of the valor, courage, and meekness of ancestors, the landscape of the trail took on what art historian Miwon Kwon calls "place-bound identity," where the trail signified much more than was visually apparent.[20]

Their own identity as Mormons was linked to the very dust of the trail; the land was more than the eye could see. Clare described its appearance as "untouched." He continued, "It looked just as it was for the pioneer. And with their memory in mind, it became sacred."[21] As they painted, the land of the pioneer migration was never neutral but continually took on a Mormon identity; furthermore, the land evoked that identity in the artists themselves. As pilgrims, travelers on a journey to a holy place, they looked at the land as hallowed ground.

THE PICTURESQUE

For the pioneer Saints, the land had a sense of picturesque beauty. Many wondered with awe at the monumental land formations they passed—such as Scotts Bluff, Ayres Natural Bridge, and Independence Rock—that were so different from the world they had left behind. They marveled at the beauty of the plains and of the mountains. For them, the American landscape was almost mythical. As twenty-first-century artists, Burton, Clare and Taylor mirrored this same sense of fascination with the splendor of the rugged natural landscape as they sketched and painted. Immersing themselves in the land, the artists painted at dusk, in the snow, in the rain, amid the dusty nothingness of Wyoming, and along the banks of the Sweetwater—often idealizing the land as they experienced much of the same awe that the pioneers felt who went before them.

Starting in 2011, Burton, Clare, and Taylor began traveling the Mormon Trail. Over the course of four years, carving out periods of weeks and months here and there, they stopped at various sites and camped to sketch and to paint en plein air. Taking its name from a French term for "in the open air,"[22] the practice of plein air painting came to prominence in the mid-nineteenth century after the invention of portable paint tubes and the box easel, sometimes called the French easel. Movements such as French Impressionism, the Barbizon School, and the Hudson River School emerged from these nineteenth-century inventions. Stylistically, plein air painters attempt to capture the actual

physical conditions of the environment, including the lighting and the atmospheric effects, gathering impressions of a singular, fleeting moment. However, unlike the Impressionists, Burton, Clare, and Taylor finished their paintings in their studios in Carmel, California; Berkeley, California; and Paradise, Utah, respectively. Still, part of the intent of these trips and the sketches they produced was to capture the essence of the land and endow the finished paintings with that same feeling of splendor and beauty that the pioneers themselves found in the picturesque land.

Josh Clare's *Lord, I Would Follow Thee* contrasts the sheer verticality of Scotts Bluff, Nebraska, with the smallness of the winding trail below and the flatness of the plains that foreground it (page 59). A midafternoon shadow creeps over the bluff, darkening it and adding to the dimensional

Josh Clare, *Lord, I Would Follow Thee*, detail.

crease marking its formation. The composition is cropped in such a way that the bluff itself seems to triumph over the sky. The intricacies of the bluff are largely abstracted, creating what appears to be one singular, massive form. With the exception of faint white wisps higher in the sky, the clouds appear low and hide shyly behind the towering natural formation that dominates the land visually, taking on the appearance of a monument.

While some accounts are harrowing, not all the experiences of the Mormon pioneers were tragic. Journal entries capture the mundane and practical toiling of daily life—finding places to wash clothes, picking wildflowers, playing music and dancing together in the evening, encountering Native Americans, hunting buffalo, traversing the seemingly never-ending muddy roads, and enduring frequent rainstorms. Often, pioneer journals describe the trek west as a great adventure, a once-in-a-lifetime experience filled with amazement, wonder, and beauty, particularly linked to an experience with the land. For nineteenth-century travelers, some of whom had crossed the Atlantic, a wagon caravan offered sights never before seen, and many journals reveal a collective sense of having experienced the grandeur of the near-mythical American West. Further, most of these accounts point to the transformative nature of the experience, traumatic or not, and attest to the forming and shaping of testimonies and collective identities as Latter-day Saints along the dusty trail, somewhere in Nebraska, while crossing the Missouri or the Platte, or in the winding hills of Emigration Canyon.

Describing Scotts Bluff, Clare said, "As the trail nears Wyoming on the western end of Nebraska, the landscape changes drastically. We caught Scotts Bluff on our trip in February of 2012, just as the sun set, turning an already inspiring sight into something very special."[23] Of the same view, Frederick Piercy wrote, "Scott's Bluffs were in view all day. They were certainly the most remarkable sight I had seen since I left England. Viewed from the distance at which I sketched them the shadows were of an intense blue,

while the rock illuminated by the setting sun partook of its gold, making a beautiful harmony of colour. They present a very singular appearance, resembling ruined palaces, castellated towers, temples and monuments."[24]

Etching of a buffalo hunt in front of Scotts Bluff, Nebraska, from Frederick Piercy's book *Route from Liverpool to Great Salt Lake Valley*, 1855.

Clare's distance from the physical rigor required of western migration may account for his aestheticizing the landscape, but his comments mirror Piercy's observations, which were not singular for his time. Describing her memory of the awe-inspiring landscape, Louisa Barnes Pratt wrote, "The grandeur of nature filled me with grateful aspirations.... So green was the grass, so delightful the wild flowers, so umbrageous the grounds on the banks of the rivers!"[25] Samuel Openshaw said he wished people of the old country could see "these wild prairies where the air is not tainted with the smoke of cities or factories, but is quiet here."[26] Such writings and reactions attest to notions grounded in nineteenth-century Romanticism, with its emphasis on the land as a source of transformative beauty. The prevalence of such descriptions throughout the contemporary accounts suggests that theories of the picturesque provided a useful lens through which early pioneers could filter and describe their new experiences.

In his essay on picturesque beauty, English clergyman and author William Gilpin wrote, "Disputes about beauty might perhaps be involved in less confusion, if a distinction were established … between those [objects], which please the eye in their *natural state;* and those, which please from some quality, capable of being *illustrated in painting.*"[27] The elements of the picturesque are not just interesting, beautiful landscapes in and of themselves but, rather, sites worthy of being transformed (and made more beautiful and more powerful) in paint. The word *picturesque* means "having the elements or qualities of a picture; suitable for a picture."[28] This definition is more nuanced than contemporary colloquial usage, which defines the picturesque as being simply quaint and pretty. Writers of the eighteenth and nineteenth century often describe the appearance of picturesque landscape in terms of variance, ruggedness, contrasts of light and dark, and—not always but very often—the inclusion of ruins. Vistas such as these inspire the viewer, who sees the land as transcendent; the viewer who looks upon the picturesque landscape (in physical or paint form) is transformed by the experience of viewing it.

Clare's description of Scotts Bluff at sunset as "very special" and representing a drastic change of scenery and Piercy's reference to the bluffs "resembling ruined palaces, castellated towers, temples and monuments" evoke the picturesque emerging from the view of monumental land formations. Thus, the landscape is picturesque both to the pioneer, who saw his own cultural heritage of castles and ruined abbeys in the rock formations, and to the contemporary viewer, who finds the picturesque in the aura of the pioneers themselves, the wagon ruts imprinted in the mud, and the fallen fragments of settlements that lie in ruin along the scenic trail.

THE SUBLIME

Beyond picturesque beauty, the paintings in the exhibition also explore a sense of the sublime, particularly as articulated by English philosopher Edmund Burke. He said, "The passion caused by the great and sublime in *nature,* when those causes operate most powerfully, is Astonishment; and astonishment is that state of the soul, in which all its motions are suspended, with some degree of horror."[29] Landscape paintings have a long history of being linked to the sublime in the way that they capture the power, danger, and even terror of nature while also evoking a sense of God's grandeur.[30] The title *Saints at Devil's Gate* itself points to the sublime in its double meaning, first referencing the location of much suffering experienced by the noted Martin handcart company and, second, as a metaphor for all of us who face adversity today.

The tumultuous, stormy sky that fills three-fourths of the picture plane in Bryan Mark Taylor's *This Too Shall Pass* (page 95) creates a sense of insignificance in the land and people below. Nature's storm overtakes and dwarfs even the mountain range. The pounding rain paired with the billowing cumulonimbus clouds tumbles into various shades of foreboding darkness from charcoal gray to near black and then suddenly bright white. The effect is one of visual loudness, capturing the uncontrollable temperamental power of nature with its unpredictability, potential for danger, and cataclysmic extremes. Differing from the sky in Clare's *Peace, Be Still* (page 39), the sky in Taylor's painting overtakes the picture plane with a sense of almost terrifying dread in the face of the awesome power of nature. Like the vastness of the sky in the painting *The Monk by the Sea* (1808–1810) by painter Caspar David Friedrich, the scale in proportion to the figure creates a sense of unsettled discomfort in the viewer.

The location depicted is Rocky Ridge as seen from a distance, a site on the Mormon Trail known for the extreme suffering of the Willie handcart company. Referencing those ill-prepared pioneers, Stegner wrote, "Their intention was

Bryan Mark Taylor, *This Too Shall Pass*, detail.

so impudent it was almost sublime." He further noted, "Signs of God's power on the exposed plains were awesome."[31] Describing a storm that hit the Edmund Ellsworth handcart company (a company traveling just ahead of the Willie and Martin companies) on July 26, 1856, Archer Walters noted, "We had not got far and it began to lightning and so on the thunders roared and about the middle of the train of hand carts the lighting struck a brother and he fell to rise no more."[32] English convert Jean Rio Griffiths Baker called the scenery along the trail "grand and terrible."[33] Sarah Maria Mousley (Cannon) wrote, "I feel my pen or thoughts inadequate to the task of portraying a true picture of the awful grandeur and beauty of these scenes."[34] In her trail journal Hannah Tapfield King observed, "We have been for some days passing 'the Rocky Mountains.' They are rather more wonderful than beautiful—yet they are certainly sublime. It seems something marvelous & mysterious that our cavalcade should pass along breaking the eternal silence of these wild places. My feelings are undefinable but there is a degree of awe & sadness about them to me."[35]

These descriptions differ from that of the picturesque. For Baker, the landscape was sublime because it was "grand and terrible." King references the sublime in writing that her "feelings are undefinable," and the inadequacy of Mousley's pen points to a failure of words in the face of great wonder, grandness, and power. So very often, words such as *awesome, awestruck, magnificent, terrible, transcendent,* and *reverence* are associated with sublime experiences. French philosopher Denis Diderot said, "All that stuns the soul, all that imprints a feeling of terror, leads to the sublime."[36] Setting out to define this characteristic in his book *The Sublime,* Philip Shaw said, "A building or a mountain may be sublime, as may a thought, a heroic deed, or a mode of expression.... Our attempts to match such grandeur necessarily fall short of the mark.... Yet somehow a sense of God's majesty is conveyed through this very failure."[37]

Josh Clare, *Peace, Be Still*, detail.

Nineteenth-century pioneers may have read Edmund Burke, whose book *A Philosophical Enquiry into the Origin of Our Ideas of the Sublime and Beautiful* had been reprinted at least ten times in America alone before the start of the Civil War.[38] For Burke, beauty and the picturesque were limited and simple; they could be comprehended and easily grasped. In contrast, the sublime was overwhelming to the point of pain, causing the mind to fail in its ability to understand. "When the prophet David contemplated the wonders of wisdom and power, which are displayed in the economy of man," Burke wrote of the sublime, "he seems to be struck with a sort of divine horror, and cries out, *fearfully and wonderfully am I made!*"[39] A similar example can be found in the Pearl of Great Price (a work of Latter-day Saint scripture) when Moses views "the world and the ends thereof, and all the children of men which are, and which were created." His response is that of befuddlement and an experience of the sublime. He says, "Now, for this cause I know that man is nothing, which thing I never had supposed."[40]

As with the picturesque, much of the writing on the sublime is understood within the tradition of the landscape. Marjorie Hope Nicolson points out that the English writers on the sublime agree that the most important "stimulus to the Sublime lay in vast objects of Nature—mountains and oceans, stars and cosmic space—all reflecting the glory of Deity."[41] Greatness, vastness, and scale (both extremely large and extremely small) can also evoke the sublime, in part because of the perspective they create. The toilings of the Mormon pioneers (as well as the trappings and cacophony of modern life) are but a distant and insignificant thing in comparison to the sky filled with a foreboding storm in *This Too Shall Pass*. In this sense, a landscape can have a sense of God's greatness, in part due to its grandeur, power, and vastness, but also in comparison to one's own human vulnerability.

SAINTS AT DEVIL'S GATE

Such framing, especially when linked to the Mormon Trail, continues to have currency and meaning for viewers today. Over the course of three decades before the arrival of the transcontinental railroad, Mormon pioneers crossed Iowa, Nebraska, and Wyoming. They descended through mountain canyons into the Salt Lake Valley, a place they thought of as Zion, described in scripture as "a land flowing with milk and honey."[42] There they would unite through shared faith to build a community out of a near-isolated desert, carving out a place for themselves in a world that was divinely sanctioned and distinctly different from the eastern United States, a place where they would grow a religion and cultivate land as a symbol of their faith.

So it is with us today, people searching for a sense of home, of belonging, and of safety. And, it is my hope as a curator that when visitors view these works, especially when the paintings are paired with the journals and reminiscences of the pioneers, words such as *beautiful, picturesque, transcendent, sublime,* and *reverence* come to mind. Because not only do many people point to the pioneers' legacy as an example, but the historical accounts also serve as metaphors for the

tumultuous journey of life itself. Such persistent travailing mirrors the times when we ourselves, like the Saints at Devil's Gate, toil, stumble, and feel ourselves as refugees, destitute wanderers without a home. Like the early Saints, we sacrifice, struggle, experience profound loss, and prevail in the messiness and heartaches of daily life. And in such times—with our vulnerability, our feelings of insignificance, our terror, our fear, and even our failures—we come to understand the greatness of God more intimately and in ways we hadn't before.

Josh Clare, Untitled, sketch (Devil's Gate, Wyoming, 2014).

For aren't we all on a journey that tries our faith, tests our courage, makes us vulnerable, and at times defeats us and blisters our soul? How many times have we looked around for holy water to quench our thirsty souls? Or stood in awe at the majesty and grandeur of God's creation—of rock formations, of small flowers, of tall and stalwart trees with thick, grounding roots—and pondered with profound gratitude our Maker? In those times, not only do Latter-day Saints of the past stand as believers at the precipice of hopelessness, pleading for rescue, for transendence, but all of us stand there as well, as saints at Devil's Gate.

"OH HOW I WISH MINE WERE A PAINTER'S PENCIL OR POET'S PEN":

Pioneer Reflections on the Landscape of the Mormon Trail
Bryon C. Andreasen

From the time of the expulsion of the Mormons from Illinois in 1846 until the arrival of the railroad in Utah in 1869, more than seventy thousand Latter-day Saints trudged across the interior of America from the Mississippi River to the Rocky Mountains.[1] In wagons and on foot they made their pilgrimage to Zion in the mountain valleys of the Great Basin. Their route became known as the Mormon Trail. Nothing in their previous experience adequately prepared these Mormon pioneers for their encounter with the western landscapes they traversed.

Today the Mormon Trail is fly-over country. In three hours, people can zoom high over a landscape that it took nineteenth-century pioneers four months or more to cross. Even those intrepid earthbound souls who brave the long drive can make the journey from Nauvoo, Illinois, to Salt Lake City in less than twenty-four hours. Hurling down the highway in the temperature-controlled cabin of a car, van, or truck, they can distract themselves with music, movies, and electronic devices as seemingly endless miles of terrain blur past the windows.

For over thirty-five years, I traversed the country by car on annual family trips to Utah from our homes "back east"—first from New York and then from Illinois. My children suffered the misfortune of having a historian for a father. No electronic devices allowed. All were to watch out the window, ponder the landscape, and use their historical imaginations.

The kids coped by inventing games. They created their own mental maps of the route, picking out landmarks that with time became family signposts on the annual journey—a favorite freeway rest stop here, a favorite truck stop there, unusual billboards, some odd natural features, the pioneer museum archway at Kearney, the smelly stockyard near Ogallala, the sculpture of Abraham Lincoln's head peering over the interstate

Some members of the author's family on top of Independence Rock, Wyoming, summer 2008.

at the summit east of Laramie, the Arctic Circle drive-in at Green River. With time the list got longer. It helped make the drive seem shorter.

I was aware that Interstate 80 tracked (more or less) the Mormon Trail in long stretches of Nebraska and down the Echo Canyon stretch in Utah. Occasionally we detoured onto Nebraska state roads past Chimney Rock and Scotts Bluff. I tried to practice what I preached. I read Wallace Stegner's classic *The Gathering of Zion: The Story of the Mormon Trail*.[2] I brought along the National Park Service's lengthy foldout map of the Mormon Pioneer Trail. I tried to imagine my great-great-great-grandmother who, at the age of nine, watched her mother die in the Iowa mud near Soap Creek during the exodus from Nauvoo in 1846. I tried to imagine her three years later as she walked from Kanesville (Council Bluffs), Iowa, to Salt Lake City, allowing her two younger sisters and new stepmother nursing an infant to ride in the wagon. I tried to imagine these experiences from the perspective of her much-tried and anxious father.[3] I wish they had left accounts of their Mormon Trail journey. But they didn't. I can only imagine their reactions to the unfamiliar geography they encountered.

Unlike my ancestors, I was familiar with the geography of the Mormon Trail landscapes before I made my first trip. Being a Utah native, high mountains, rugged canyons, wild rock formations, and arid sagebrush-covered expanses were nothing new. Hollywood movies, television shows, documentaries, and colorful photographs and illustrations in picture books, magazines, and atlases visually introduced me to eastern sections of the trail that included the plains and prairies of Nebraska and Iowa. Accurate foreknowledge made my trip more of a confirmatory adventure—and less of the adventure of surprising discoveries that I imagine the trip was for my forebears.

Before leaving Nauvoo, Mormon leaders tried to acquire accurate foreknowledge.[4] They studied government maps and reports. Later, emigrant guidebooks and popular travel

accounts were more broadly available to inform the imaginations of rank-and-file pioneers. But these sources had no photographs (that technology was still in its infancy), and during the earliest years, artistic renderings of sites along the trail were few. Left with crude maps and mere words on paper, soon-to-be travelers simply could not fully anticipate the landscapes they would face.

The landscape of the first part of the trail—the nearly 265-mile stretch across southern Iowa—was a seemingly endless succession of hills punctuated by streams and rivers that in

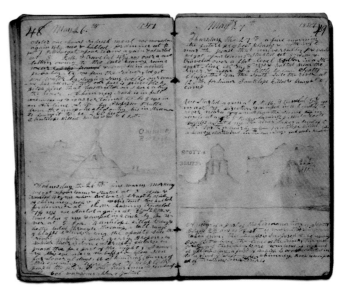

Sketches of Chimney Rock and Scotts Bluffs from the 1847 diary of Appleton Milo Harmon.

spring seasons overflowed and turned the trail into a miring, muddy mess. Those fleeing Nauvoo in 1846 were the primary users of this portion of the trail. Latter-day Saints began crossing the Mississippi River in the snow and ice of February. Each successive month, more families followed. By the late-summer heat of early September, several hundred Mormon families still remained in Nauvoo. These Latter-day Saints were forced across the river at gunpoint. In all, almost fifteen thousand made it across across Iowa that year. On reaching and crossing the Missouri River on Iowa's western border, the first pioneer companies established a way station they named Winter Quarters (present-day Florence, Nebraska). Here and in surrounding areas, the Saints endured a brutal winter as they regrouped and prepared for a longer trip the following season.[5]

The second part of the Mormon Trail covered the 1,032 miles between Winter Quarters and the Salt Lake Valley.[6] Going west, landscapes shifted from the sometimes-soggy, flat grass prairies along the Platte River in eastern Nebraska to the more arid plains of North Platte River country in western Nebraska and eastern Wyoming. Here the pioneers began encountering dramatic western landscapes of bluffs and buttes. Such features became more pronounced, accentuated by strange rock formations, along central Wyoming's Sweetwater River. Then beyond the Green River came the towering mountains and rugged canyons that confounded the path to the Great Salt Lake.

Across the entire trail, the sheer vastness of the landscapes was breathtaking. The deafening silence of seemingly still emptiness evoked feelings of loneliness and insignificance. The topography seemed alien, so different from the familiar scenes of their homelands. Panoramas of desolate wild scenery challenged the pioneers' comprehension and their descriptive abilities. Sharing the lamentation of many, twenty-nine-year-old Sarah Maria Mousley (Cannon) wrote in her journal, while in sight of Chimney Rock: "Oh how I wish mine were a painter's pencil or poet's pen. I would portray if possible the beauty of the scenes through which we have been called to pass."[7]

Writing a century later, Wallace Stegner remarked, "The fabled [trail] landmarks made tourists out of pilgrims, bad poets out of good diarists."[8] Indeed, pioneers' diaries and memoirs document how they signposted their mental trail maps with physical landmarks in much the same way my children did while traveling the freeway generations later. My ancestors did not leave trail accounts, but fortunately many pioneers did (including ancestors of the artists whose work is featured in the exhibition *Saints at Devil's Gate*).

Many pioneer accounts seem cursory. Others are vivid and full of ruminations. In the exhibition, the words of some who made the memorable journey along the Mormon Trail between 1847 and 1869 are matched with stunning artwork. Stegner's verdict on pioneer poetry aside, their words reveal an array of reactions to the physical environment.

How pioneers experienced landscapes depended on a variety of things: the mode of transportation they used, their age and sex, the particular company with which they traveled, and the year and season when they undertook the trek. Regardless of these circumstances, however, their writings show that while landscapes could arouse discouragement and fear over the daunting physical obstacles they posed, they could also evoke awe and admiration for their beauty at the same time. Sentiments of hardship, misery, and sacrifice were recurrent but not constant; expressions of happiness, humor, joy, exhilaration, and a sense of spiritual reverence are common. "We were led many times [to] admire and adore the God of nature who in his mighty power formed such wonderful curiosities," wrote Caroline Barnes Crosby, reflecting the sentiments expressed in many records. "Marvelous are thy works thou Lord of hosts."[9]

The journey west to Zion was the adventure of a lifetime. It was a defining event in the life of every Latter-day Saint who made it. Each pioneer had to come to terms with the landscape of the Mormon Trail. The journey was both an ordeal of physical and emotional endurance and an exhilarating encounter with wild settings and a physical world foreign to all. Through hardship and beauty, suffering and wonderment, the trail landscape tested character, stretched minds, and expanded understandings.

It's a shame these landscapes are now fly-over country, that so many travelers today race past them without a thoughtful pause. If these paintings kindle in some a desire to slow down and take in the landscape, to exercise historical imagination while infusing the views with fresh, personal meaning, the exhibition will have been a success.

SAINTS AT DEVIL'S GATE

EXHIBITION

THE MORMON TRAIL

📍 LOCATIONS PAINTED

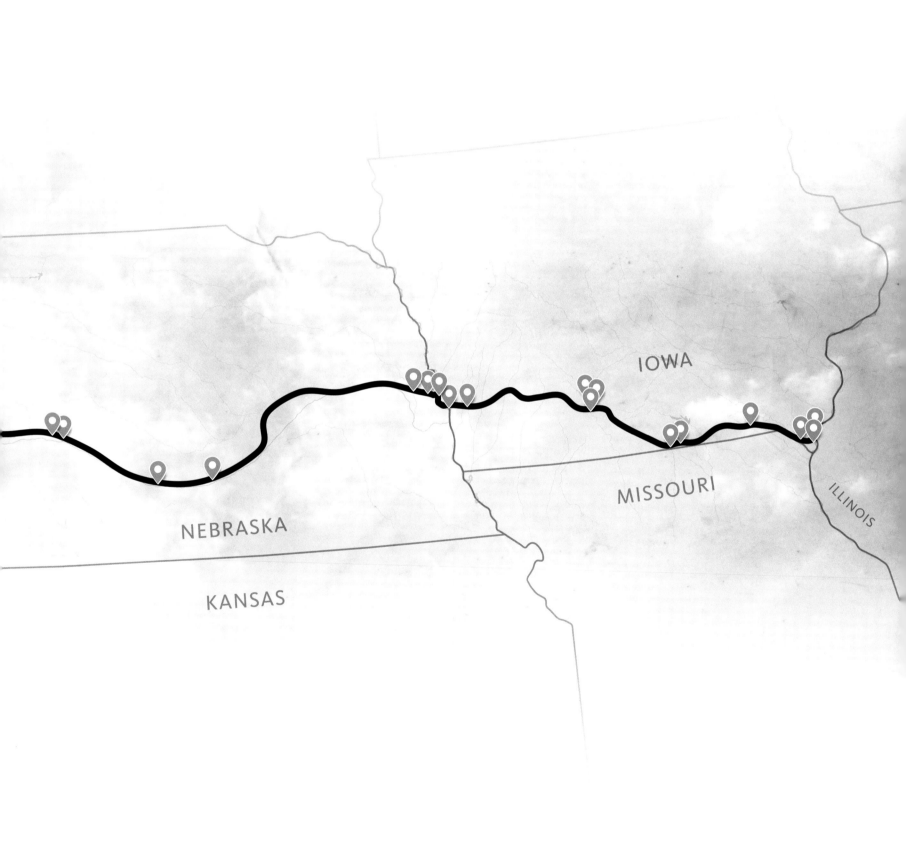

John Burton
Nauvoo, Illinois
2016, oil on canvas

" [We] crossed the [Mississippi] River on the ice…. The last wagon crossing the river broke through…. My husband in helping to get the wagon from the river got very wet and took a violent cold that settled on his lungs from which he never recovered. He died six weeks later and was buried by the roadside between two large trees to mark his resting place."[1]

Harriet Amelia Decker Little (Hanks)
Age 19, February 1846, exodus across Iowa. Reminiscence, 1914.

" I went with my family to the [Mississippi] River to cross over into Iowa. We waited a while for a boat. At length we went on board of an old small boat and started over, the wind being quite high & the river rough. While on the water I beheld the most heart rending and dangerous scenes that I was ever called to witness…. [*Stout described seeing a boat full of Saints sink while crossing the river.*] They gave themselves up to the watery grave and all was hushed and the boat went down. In a few minutes we saw them scattered on the surface of the water…in silent & frightful anticipation of soon leaving this world of fears & disappointments. Some were on feather beds, sticks of wood, lumber or anything they could get hold of and were tossed & sported on the water at the mercy of the cold and unrelenting waves."[2]

Hosea Stout
Age 35, February 1846, exodus across Iowa. Trail journal.

LOOKING BACK
Bryan Mark Taylor
Montrose, Iowa
2015, oil on canvas

“I left Nauvoo for the last time perhaps in this life. I looked upon the temple & city of Nauvoo as I retired from it & felt to ask the Lord to preserve it as a monument of the sacrifice of his Saints."[3]

Wilford Woodruff
Age 39, May 1846, exodus across Iowa. Trail journal.

“We left the Mississippi about noon. We ascended the bluffs. Here we halted, and took a farewell view of our delightful city, that we had seen and helped to rear from its infancy. We also beheld the magnificent temple, rearing its lofty tower towards the heavens, which speaks volumes in honor of the wisdom and greatness of our martyred prophet…. We also took a farewell look at our homes. Whilst looking and pondering upon all this, I felt grateful to my heavenly father … and asked His protecting care over us on our journey. Yea, my heart swelled within me, because of the things which I beheld."[4]

Newel Knight
Age 45, April 1846, exodus across Iowa. Trail journal.

Josh Clare
Near Sugar Creek Camp, Iowa
2015, oil on canvas

"While traveling through the state of Iowa with six hundred immigrants with hand-carts and the dust of harvest weather four or five inches deep, the sun pouring down on our heads and the perspiration and wet dust streaming down our faces and in our throats, choking us so we could hardly breathe and tantalized by the people coming out of their houses and telling us that was a...hard way to serve the Lord, and...the young hoodlums would go ahead of the company to the next river or creek to ridicule our wives and daughters who had to raise their dresses out of the water to wade the streams as there was not many bridges."[5]

John Watkins
Age 22, English convert, late summer 1856, Edward Martin handcart company. Reminiscence, date uncertain.

"I had worn my English bonnet this day and the sun scorched my face— It felt on fire— Mr. Shores took particular pains to caution us against getting our complexions spoilt— Even Anne he talked to about covering her arms— He said he hated to see a woman's fine skin burned up ... I mounted my post to drive the horses...I feel sure few women (English) dare drive over where I have gone, and it has shaken my nerves into a muddle."[6]

Hannah Tapfield King
Age 46, English convert, late spring 1853, Claudius V. Spencer company. Reminiscence, circa 1864–1872.

" Suddenly the loud thunders began to roar! Fierce lightnings flashed! I knew my tent would not shed rain, and I dreaded the consequences of a hard shower more than I ever did in my life. I prayed most fervently that the storm might pass over and do us no harm! Suddenly the clouds began to disperse, the thunder rumbled in the distance. I looked abroad and saw the clear sky. I felt a glow of gratitude I shall long remember."[7]

Louisa Barnes Pratt
Age 43, summer 1846, exodus across Iowa. Reminiscence, 1850–1880.

" Mr. Sessions overtakes me today at Richardson's point. Yesterday I felt bad. I was not well, and I and our things were scattered on account of our heavy load and bad roads and were in nine different places. We are all together now but our cow."[8]

Martha (Patty) Bartlett Sessions (Parry)
Age 51, March 1846, exodus across Iowa. Trail journal.

ARTIST PERSPECTIVE The forced migration out of Illinois and into Iowa was extremely painful for that first group of Saints, far more traumatic than I'll ever understand. I wanted to capture some of the feelings of despair and grief they must have experienced as they left their homes as refugees and as they left the comforts of their beautiful city of Nauvoo. –JC

UPS AND DOWNS
Bryan Mark Taylor
Locust Creek, Iowa
2015, oil on canvas

"Yesterday we travelled over the most intolerable roads! It was a query in my mind how the first company, going as they did early in the spring, ever forced their way through so much mud! I was led to exclaim, what is there in all the world, the Mormons will not attempt to do?"[9]

Louisa Barnes Pratt
Age 43, June 1846, exodus across Iowa. Reminiscence, 1850–1880.

"Thus far have had good roads considering the heavy rains. This is I think the most beautiful country that I ever saw. The prairies are rolling with streams of water plenty. The inhabitants are mostly people from the eastern states and generally kind to us.… There is little fear of losing our road as there is but one."[10]

Lorenzo Brown
Age 23, May 1846, exodus across Iowa. Reminiscence, circa 1856.

ARTIST PERSPECTIVE
Today Iowa is a bucolic array of farms and gently rolling hills. However, when the first Mormon pioneers traveled this area, it was daunting. Travel through Iowa took much longer than they anticipated. Wagon wheels constantly became stuck in the muddy dips of the road and had to be dug out continually as they crossed the rolling contours of the Iowa terrain. –BMT

John Burton

Locust Creek, Iowa
2016, oil on canvas

CURATOR'S RESPONSE

THE CALL OF ZION The birds in Burton's *Faith (All Is Well)* echo the feeling of migration of the Mormon pilgrims. As the birds take flight, they seem to lift heavenward. Such was the belief of many Mormon pioneers—that through their migration to the West, to Zion, they would reach a promised land (even if the idealized utopia was, in reality, more human than heaven). The title of the painting is paired with the lyrics of William Clayton's pioneer anthem "Come, Come, Ye Saints" (originally titled "All Is Well"), which acts as a beckoning call for the gathering. Said Wallace Stegner, "For every early Saint, crossing the plains to Zion in the Valleys of the Mountains was not merely a journey but a rite of passage, the final, devoted, enduring act that brought one into the Kingdom.... And to successive generations who did not personally experience it, it has continued to have sanctity as legend and myth."[11] Accessing that legacy of faith, both in paint and in person, was exactly what Burton was seeking to do with this project, that through his pilgrimage, he could glean from the past a structure of faith for today. –LAH

"Continued to rain all day very heavy. The camp is very disagreeable and muddy.... In the evening...the band met in the tent and played on the violins. All the time we were playing, the lightning occasionally broke forth from the N. W. [Northwest]. At 8 o'clock we dispersed just as the storm approached.... The rain beat through the wagon covers & drenched families and effects. It was the most severe storm we have experienced and with such weather it seems impossible to preserve our little clothing & provisions from being spoiled. But in the midst of all the camp all are cheerful and happy and there are but few sick.... This morning Ellen Kimball came to me & wished me much joy. She said Diantha [Clayton's wife] has got a son.... This morning I composed a new song, "All is Well" ["Come, Come, Ye Saints"]. I feel to thank my heavenly father for my boy and pray that he will spare and preserve his life and that of his mother.... O Lord bless thine handmaid and fill her with thy Spirit. Make her healthy that her life may be prolonged and that we may live long upon the earth to honor the cause of truth."[12]

William Clayton
Age 31, English convert, April 6 and 15, 1846, exodus across Iowa.
Trail journal.

Josh Clare
Mount Pisgah, Iowa
2014, oil on canvas

CURATOR'S RESPONSE

TITLES AS NARRATIVE Depicting a frozen brook, Clare's painting captures the sense of cold and emptiness within the land. The close-cropped composition focuses on the brightness of the snow against the winter grass. Winter has long been used as a metaphor for human struggle, but Clare pairs this barren scene with 2 Corinthians 12:9–10, in which the Lord states, "My grace is sufficient for thee: for my strength is made perfect in weakness," to which Paul replies, "Therefore I take pleasure in infirmities, in reproaches, in necessities, in persecutions, in distresses for Christ's sake: for when I am weak, then am I strong."

Throughout the exhibition, Burton, Clare, and, to a lesser extent, Taylor use the titles of their paintings to link a narrative to the land as a way of drawing out deeper meaning. The titles expose a sense of history and faith that, for them, still exists in the physicality of the Mormon Trail— memories manifested in streams, brooks, dust, and rocks. –LAH

"Drove about 3 miles & came to a house the last one on our route. We thus leave the abodes of civilization to go forth as wanderers on the Earth without homes not knowing on what part of the continent we might be permitted to stop, some asserting our destination was Salt Lake Valley, some that we were going to some point on the upper Mississippi…while I believe it was thought by many that we should locate ourselves on Van Couvers [Vancouver] Island at the mouth of the Columbia River which is British Territory. I have often laughed at an observation made to me by a settler with whom I chanced to meet one day on the prairie. His inquiry was what part are you expecting to locate in. I answered in all sincerity, I really do not know sir. His reply was, When I leave with my family not knowing where I expect to stop, any person is at liberty to call me a damned fool."[13]

Lorenzo Brown
Age 23, May 28, 1846, exodus across Iowa. Reminiscence, circa 1856.

MOUNT PISGAH OVERLOOK
Bryan Mark Taylor
Mount Pisgah, Iowa
2014, oil on canvas

Church leaders looked to the future needs of thousands of Saints who would follow them west to the Missouri River by establishing temporary settlements in Iowa. The largest was at Mount Pisgah—named for the Old Testament peak where Moses viewed the promised land. In the Iowan Mount Pisgah, enclosed fields provided food, and simple buildings provided shelter for Saints needing to recuperate and replenish. Mount Pisgah was "the first place where I felt willing in my heart to stay at, since I left Nauvoo," declared newly called apostle Ezra T. Benson. Here, officers of the United States Army first recruited members of the Mormon Battalion. After six years of use, the Saints closed the settlement in 1852.[14] –BCA

" I stopped my carriage on the top of a rolling prairie and I had a most splendid view. I could stand and gaze to the east, west, north & south & behold the Saints pouring out & gathering like clouds from the hills & dales, grove & prairie with their teams, waggons, flocks, & herds, by hundreds & thousands as it were until it looked like the movements of a great nation."[15]

Wilford Woodruff
Age 39, June 1846, exodus across Iowa. Trail journal.

" The wind is blowing a heavy gale: it seems as though the very heavens would come down to earth! The tent is pinned down, or it would be carried away. The elements are in great commotion, and my mind is dark and dismal! I think, 'What if we have to wander forty years in the wilderness, as the children of Israel did!'"[16]

Louisa Barnes Pratt
Age 43, June 1846, exodus across Iowa. Reminiscence, 1850–1880.

Josh Clare
Mount Pisgah, Iowa
2015, oil on canvas

"Riding about three or four miles through beautiful prairies, I came suddenly to some round and sloping hills, grassy and crowned with beautiful groves of timber;… on the west, rolled a main branch of Grand River, with its rich bottoms of alternate forest and prairie. As I approached this lovely scenery several deer and wolves, being startled at the sight of me, abandoned the place and bounded away till lost from my sight amid the groves. Being pleased and excited at the varied beauty before me, I cried out, 'This is Mount Pisgah.'"[17]

Parley P. Pratt
Age 39, spring 1846, exodus across Iowa. Reminiscence, circa 1854–1856.

"This place is called Mount Pisgah and is a very beautiful situation; the prairie rolling and rich, skirted with beautiful groves of timber on the main fork of Grand River."[18]

William Clayton
Age 31, English convert, May 26, 1846, exodus across Iowa. Trail journal.

"Came on through Pisgah. Road very muddy. Nothing seemed very pleasant to me…. Crossed a branch of Grand River. Very bad bridge. Had to ford. A few miserable looking log cabins in P[isgah], and some of the raggedest children I ever saw."[19]

Caroline Barnes Crosby
Age 41, May 1848, Willard Richards company. Trail journal.

PRESS ON

Josh Clare

Western Iowa

2014, oil on canvas

"There was a dreadful hill to climb as we drove off the boat, deep mud, and at the top thick woods. It was dark, and we dared not drive on. Had no place to pitch the tent. So there we must remain till morning, mosquitoes beyond endurance. I, with a raging fever, the four children with me on the bed."[20]

Louisa Barnes Pratt

Age 44, September 1847, exodus across Iowa. Reminiscence, 1850–1880.

"It seems hardly worthwhile to write every day's journal for they consist all the time of thunder storms—mud holes, making bridges—getting wet thro' beds and all. I note down some of these, and then add how I enjoy my carriage bed & how thankful I am for my many blessings."[21]

Hannah Tapfield King

Age 46, English convert, June 1853, Claudius V. Spencer company. Reminiscence, circa 1864–1872.

PEACE, BE STILL

Josh Clare

Council Bluffs, Iowa

2016, oil on canvas

"Traveled through a beautiful country where we could stand and gaze upon the prairies as far as the eye could carry, even until the prairies themselves seemed to meet the sky on all sides, without being able to see a house. Thought how many thousands of people are there in England who have scarce room to breathe and not enough to eat. Yet, all this good land lying dormant, except for the prairie grass to grow and decay."[22]

Samuel Openshaw

Age 22, English convert, August 1856, Edward Martin handcart company. Trail journal.

"The Missouri, just one big river of mud, flowing out of somewhere, sluggishly past, and on into a nowhere! 'However can we wash our clothes in this,' was my uppermost thought and I was really greatly relieved when I found that all the washing was to be done at a spring situated in a group of trees, near the camp."[23]

Amelia Eliza Slade (Bennion)
Age 9, English convert, early summer 1864, Warren S. Snow company. Reminiscence, date uncertain.

"A cold dreary winter was before us. I hired a man to build me a sod cave; he took the turf from the earth, laid it up, covered it with willow brush and sods; built a chimney of the same. I hung up a blanket for a door, had three lights of glass to emit light. I built a fire, drew up my rocking chair before it, and that moment felt as rich as some persons (who have never suffered for want of a house) would to be moved into a costly building. Thus we learn to prize enjoyments by sacrifices."[24]

Louisa Barnes Pratt
Age 44, winter 1846–1847, Winter Quarters camp. Reminiscence, 1850–1880.

ARTIST PERSPECTIVE I found it difficult to capture the essence of what I felt at Winter Quarters. Absorbed within the city of Omaha itself, modern structures have taken over, and few signs remain of the historic outpost. One evening, however, I walked along the river and observed the fires of groups camped along the Missouri. This simple reference immediately transported me to an earlier time when similar campfires provided needed warmth and comfort to the weary Saints on their westward trek. –BMT

Josh Clare
Winter Quarters, Nebraska
2015, oil on canvas

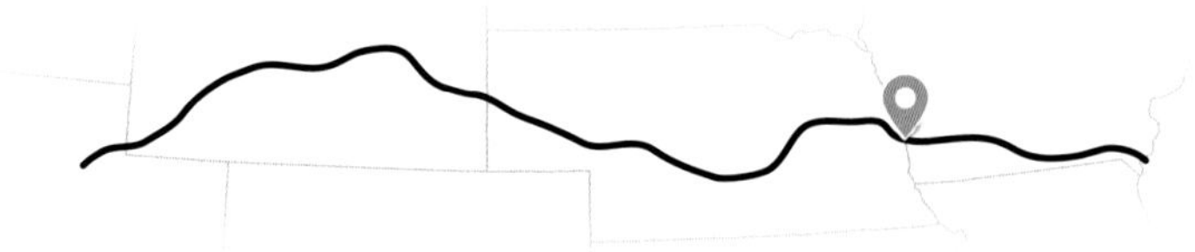

CURATOR'S RESPONSE

CONTEMPORARY LENS The contemporary context of this project is no more obvious than in *Temple Hill.* This is one of the few paintings and sketches to include markers of now—telephone lines, asphalt-paved roads, sidewalks, tree-lined streets, and homes. Such settlement stands in stark contrast to the sod cave Louisa Barnes Pratt described in her journal (page 40).

While much of the land painted by Burton, Clare, and Taylor carefully crops out civilization and frames the landscape as isolated and alone, Clare's inclusion of such modernization bespeaks the transformation of many pioneer stops into established towns and cities. Further, it points out the construct implicit in the paintings themselves. The collective works are idealized depictions cropped to maintain the view of the land as intact, the trail still accessible. –LAH

" Soon we are where the Saints had their Winter Quarters when they were driven from civilization. Here were relics of different natures; a house that Brigham Young had lived in, a well that Heber C. Kimball had dug and the remains of dugouts, camping places and other sacred memories of gone-by time."[25]

John Lingren
Age 18, Swedish convert, spring 1863, John F. Sanders company. Reminiscence, 1893.

" We now hastened our departure from Winter Quarters, glad to get away from that inhospitable place with life even, for we did not think we should have had even that if we had remained much longer."[26]

George Washington Hill
Age 25, summer 1847, Abraham O. Smoot–George B. Wallace company. Reminiscence, 1878.

Josh Clare

Elkhorn River Crossing, Nebraska
2016, oil on canvas

STARTING THE JOURNEY IN EAR-NEST The Elkhorn River was the first natural obstacle faced by the pioneers after leaving Winter Quarters. Wagons rendezvoused here to ferry across the water and then reassemble in groups on the other side. It was common to spend several days here preparing for the long trek along the meandering Platte River, which was just visible in the distance. Elation at having begun the journey is reflected in glowing descriptions of the landscape in many pioneer accounts. "The country in the neighborhood of the Elk Horn is one of the most beautiful I ever saw," gushed William Clayton. Hannah Tapfield King mused: "The fireflies are beautiful here. They are like diamond dust over every thing at night."[27] –BCA

"We found this to be a pleasant place to camp. The river abounded with fish, and we found a variety of wild fruit, such as gooseberries, currants and wild grapes. The men and boys indulged in bathing and fishing; the women and girls, in gathering fruit. One boy caught a fish which weighed eighteen pounds and he could not pull it out of the water. One of the men got a gun and shot it for the boy."[28]

Henry Stokes
Age 33, English convert, August 6, 1862, Henry W. Miller company. Trail journal.

"We made our way as best we could to the Elkhorn River to the place where we could be organized for the journey. Here we had to make a raft of logs to ferry ourselves over the river. I assisted to ferry the whole of the companies, consisting of some five hundred and sixty wagons, over this river on a log raft, accomplishing this feat without accident of any note. We were here organized into A[braham] O. Smoot's hundred, Major [Samuel] Russell's fifty, and Samuel Turnbow's ten."[29]

George Washington Hill
Age 25, summer 1847, Abraham O. Smoot–George B. Wallace company. Reminiscence, 1878.

Josh Clare

Near Fort Kearny, Nebraska

2016, oil on canvas

"Elizabeth [Meneary Scott] in one wagon had sons 4–6 and 2 daughters 8–10 and a new baby too. [I] had a son [Hyrum] 22 months old and Sarah [Ann Willis]…had a son [Joseph] 2 months old in her arms. Yet here we… who have been raised in luxury, are bravely trying to drive a mule team across the plains, holding our babies. We take turns driving. You can just imagine we three women climbing in and out over wagon wheels to cook on the camp fire and wash clothes."[30]

Mary Pugh Scott
Age 26, English convert, circa June 1848, Heber C. Kimball company. Reminiscence, 1877.

"Started at half past eight o'clock. The weather is extremely hot which makes it hard traveling. Stopped at one o'clock, but moved no farther today. It would truly be an amusing and interesting scene if the people of the old country could have a bird's eye view of us when in camp; to see everyone busy—some fetching water, others gathering buffalo chips, some cooking and so forth upon these wild prairies where the air is not tainted with the smoke of cities or factories, but is quiet here. One may see a creek at a distance and start and travel one hour towards it, yet seems no nigher than you did when you started."[31]

Samuel Openshaw
Age 22, English convert, September 16, 1856, Edward Martin handcart company. Trail journal.

ARTIST PERSPECTIVE It's perfectly impossible to imagine traveling twelve miles a day when you're traveling sixty miles per hour in an air-conditioned vehicle, but I tried to incorporate into this painting something of the heat and the dust and the long days the Saints must have experienced. -JC

" One evening as we prepared to stop for the night a large herd of buffalo came thundering toward us. It sounded like thunder at first, then the big black animals came straight for our carts. We were so scared that we were rooted to the ground. One of the captains, seeing what was going on, ran for the carts ... to make a path for the steady stream of animals and let them go through. They went past us like a train roaring along. I'm sure that but for the quick thinking of these men that many of us would have been trampled to death.... After they had gone somebody called out that the cattle had gone with them. This was our only supply of meat, so the men started right out after them. The men on foot soon lost the sight of the herd."[32]

Emma James (Johnson)
Age 17, English convert, September 1856, James G. Willie handcart company. Reminiscence, date uncertain.

" In the course of my walk I saw a large buffalo which had been to the river for drink. He was just rising the bank as I came in sight of him. It appeared that his curiosity was as much aroused as mine. He gazed at me for a moment, as I did at him. Then shaking his head and switching his tail, [he] started toward me in great haste, but as there were several deep gulfs between us I was not much afraid of his reaching before I could gain the wagons, however I concluded it was best for me to be leaving.... Yesterday we found several buffalo skulls with inscriptions on them which gave us intelligence from the forward co[mpanie]s. We found they were a month wanting four days before us."[33]

Caroline Barnes Crosby
Age 41, August 1848, Willard Richards company. Trail journal.

HISTORICAL CONTEXT **BISON ENCOUNTERS** Almost every pioneer had something to say about buffalo (offically called bison). Along with descriptions of American Indians, this animal is one of the most remarked-on topics in journals and memoirs. Most had never seen buffalo before. Stories of leaving messages inscribed on buffalo skulls are true. Thomas Bullock, for instance, recorded in his journal on June 11, 1847: "I wrote on a skull direction for the next Saints, planting it near my wagon."[34] -BCA

FLAT AND WIDE
Bryan Mark Taylor
Platte River, Nebraska
2015, oil on canvas

" Encamped near the Platte River having passed the beautifulest scenery my eyes ever rested upon…. The wild flowers beautiful to behold, the air redolent with their odor, the calm still waters of beautiful lakes all serving alike to awake an adoration to that God at whose word we have left the happy scenes of childhood years to repair to the mountains with the Saints of light…. Oh how I wish mine were a painter's pencil or a poet's pen. I would portray if possible the beauty of the scenes through which we have been called to pass."[35]

Sarah Maria Mousley (Cannon)
Age 29, July and August 1857, Jacob Hofheins company.
Trail journal.

" We have had the Platte River by us for the past week. It is very pretty—full of little islands— Oh! I can write no more. The mosquitoes drive me mad!"[36]

Hannah Tapfield King
Age 46, English convert, August 3, 1853, Claudius V. Spencer company. Reminiscence, circa 1864–1872.

SEASONAL DISSONANCE The Mormon pioneers would not have known the frozen Platte River as depicted in Burton's painting. Traversing the land in wagons and handcarts could only be done safely in certain seasons of the year, and even the latest of companies, the Willie and Martin, passed by the Platte without snow. That said, dealing with varied weather conditions was a significant part of the journey for every pioneer, many of whom were out in the elements for the first time in their lives. Pioneer journals report routinely on the weather—the scorching sun, seemingly constant rain and thunderstorms, gusting winds, and sometimes, falling snow and bitter cold. Exposure in turn led to other problems, such as frostbite, sunstroke, and insect- and water-borne illnesses.

The seasonal dissonance depicted in *Impossible Is Possible* reveals the amenities available to Burton, Clare, and Taylor, who could travel in the warmth of their cars regardless of the weather. The artists did, however, hike into and camp at trail sites in all seasons of the year to better appreciate the changing landscapes and the physical trials of those who traveled the trail.

As such, their painting of the trail isn't a re-creation of the exact trek, mirroring the conditions and staying true to the period. Rather, the project is a tribute to their ancestors and a bearing witness to the physical locations through eyes of modern-day Mormons. –LAH

IMPOSSIBLE IS POSSIBLE
John Burton
Platte River, Nebraska
2016, oil on canvas

" Travelled 12 miles, according to William Clayton's Roadometer, attached this morning. The valley thro' which we have this day travelled may aptly be called the Valley of Dry Bones from the immense number of bleached buffalo bones. A young buffalo [was] killed & brought into camp. Lightning in the north west—dark clouds."[37]

Thomas Bullock
Age 30, English convert, May 12, 1847, Brigham Young 1847 pioneer company. Trail journal.

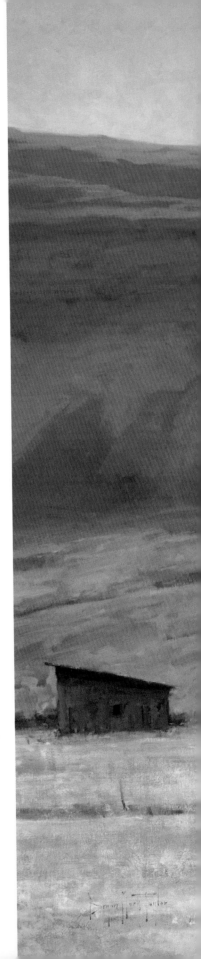

DWELLING AT CHIMNEY ROCK
Bryan Mark Taylor
Chimney Rock, Nebraska
2014, oil on canvas

" A long day's travel! This day these sublime bluffs in view all day!— They plainly speak a designer—tho' ages must have rolled along since that design was carried out."

" The Bluff ruins … are very beautiful— I should like to have an explanation about them—but I suppose none know their history— They stand out in bold relief with a silent eloquence that speaks trumpet-tongued to every thinking mind— There they are looking eternally silent."[38]

Hannah Tapfield King
Age 46, English convert, August 3 and 5, 1853, Claudius V. Spencer company. Reminiscence, circa 1864–1872.

" We camped at the foot of Chimney Rock. This is a large mound with a rock sticking up in the center like a chimney about two hundred and fifty feet high. Here many of our camp went on to the top of the mound and found the names of some of the pioneers that was ahead of us, for they had passed there some time before. Here my husband wrote his name on the rock with red keal, also my name and the names of his other wives that was with us and our children's names."[39]

Sarah DeArmon Pea Rich
Age 32, August 1, 1847, Charles C. Rich company. Reminiscence, circa 1890–1893.

John Burton
Chimney Rock, Nebraska
2016, oil on canvas

❝ Passed Chimney Rock, which is a rock that rises in the form of a monument or chimney and can be seen at a distance. We continued our journey as quick as we possibly could. The cold increasing upon us. It is severe nights and mornings. Our provisions are running out very fast so allowance has been one pound per day."[40]

Samuel Openshaw
Age 22, English convert, October 3, 1856, Edward Martin handcart company. Trail journal.

❝ We are in sight of Chimney Rock, a cliff of sand looking like a tomb on the other side of the river, or an old courthouse. Go over the bluffs. Camp on the river."[41]

Martha (Patty) Bartlett Sessions (Parry)
Age 52, July 29, 1847, Daniel Spencer–Perrigrine Sessions company. Trail journal.

CURATOR'S RESPONSE   **SHARED VISTAS** Chimney Rock was one of the most monumental landmarks on early trail maps, and its appearance is noted in many journals of the time. The towering presence of rock remains a spectacular vista, with its spire rising dramatically heavenward and standing majestically in the vast landscape. Burton was drawn to Chimney Rock as "a metaphor for the temple," which he described as architecturally being almost the same form.[42] As with any historic landmark, it is at this clearly marked point that one can stop and feel time conflated, experiencing the world as those who have gone before experienced it, echoing a shared sense of awe. Describing a similar experience with history-laden land, art historian Lucy Lippard in *The Lure of the Local* said she had "a 'vision' of the entire history of the place [that] rose from the ground at me—not in pictures or in narrative form, but in an indescribable whole, a burst of land, history, culture that *was* the place."[43] –LAH

Josh Clare
Scotts Bluff, Nebraska
2016, oil on canvas

**ROUTE FROM LIVERPOOL TO GREAT
SALT LAKE VALLEY** Frederick Piercy
was the eighth of nine children born in
Portsea, Hampshire, England. He joined
the Church of Jesus Christ of Latter-day
Saints on March 23, 1848, and a year
later, he married Angelina Hawkins, also
a convert. When Piercy was twenty
and his wife was expecting their first
child, he left for a short mission to Paris,
France. In addition to proselytizing, he
produced artwork and can be considered a predecessor to the Paris art
missionaries who came years later.

Piercy was an artist known for portrai-
ture and landscapes, and he exhibited
at the Royal Academy of Arts and at
the Suffolk Street Gallery of the Society of British Artists in London prior to
leaving for the Salt Lake Valley. In 1853,
then twenty-three years old, Piercy left
England aboard the emigrant ship *Jer-
sey*, which was headed for New Orleans.
He and James Linforth, an editor for the
Mormon newspaper *Millennial Star*, published a collection of engravings and
woodcuts made from Piercy's drawings, paintings, and journals in the book
*Route from Liverpool to Great Salt Lake
Valley*. Instead of remaining in Utah like
many others, Piercy returned to England shortly after his trip. By April 1857,
after refusing to return to the Salt Lake
Valley at the behest of both Brigham
Young and Orson Pratt, Piercy and his
wife left the Mormon faith.[44] –LAH

❝ Elder Alexander Badlam and myself explored Scott's
Bluffs from top to bottom for about 10 miles. They had
many grand formations of nature. In some places we
rolled off large rocks of near a ton's weight that would
go thundering down the mountains & into the vale
beneath, leveling the cedars to the earth & starting the
wolves from their hiding places as it bounded on its way
for half a mile from its starting point."[45]

Wilford Woodruff
Age 43, August 14, 1850, Wilford Woodruff company. Trail journal.

❝ Scott's Bluffs were in view all day. They were certainly
the most remarkable sight I had seen since I left England.
Viewed from the distance at which I sketched them the
shadows were of an intense blue, while the rock illuminated by the setting sun partook of its gold, making a
beautiful harmony of colour. They present a very singular appearance, resembling ruined palaces, castellated
towers, temples and monuments."[46]

Frederick Piercy
Age 23, English convert, July 1853, Daniel A. Miller–John W. Cooley
company. Reminiscence, circa 1854–1855.

THE PATH TO IMMORTAL

John Burton

Guernsey, Wyoming

2016, oil on canvas

" We took the new road up North Platte. Our company consisted of about ten men at that time and four wagons, and we were all strangers to the road and country.... [We were] all tired and almost famishing for water. Strong men cried for water. Some rocks near the road drew my attention, and when I had got to the top of one of those large rocks, I reached down in the top of a large one that was hollow, and to my great joy and to the joy of our company, I found a few gallons of water that had been deposited by the rain, which enabled us to continue our search. When I found the water in the rock, the story of Moses came to my mind, and I felt to acknowledge the hand of the Lord in our behalf."[47]

Noah Brimhall

Age 24, summer 1850, unknown company. Reminiscence, circa 1900–1910.

Bryan Mark Taylor

Guernsey, Wyoming

2014, oil on canvas

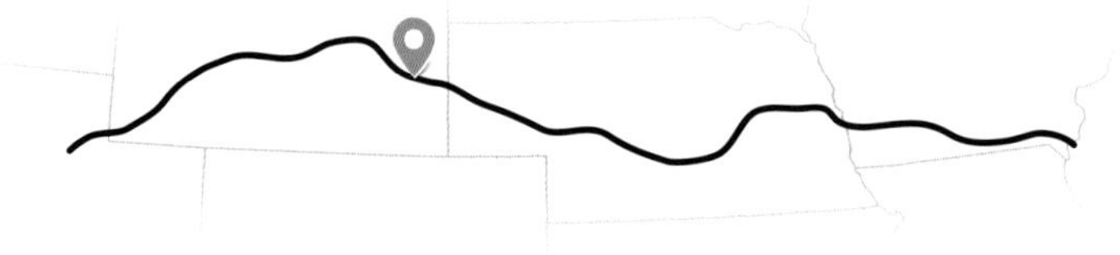

ARTIST PERSPECTIVE

There are few authentic markings from the westward pioneer migration that remain visible on the trail today. One of them is an impressive and memorable section of the trail found in Guernsey, Wyoming, which bears the marks of deep wagon ruts carved into the sandstone. These marks remain etched into the earth as a testament to the strength and perseverance of thousands. I wondered how many creaking wagons passed through this part of the trail. I imagined the first wagon companies blazing the rough trail and pioneers on subsequent teams of wagons grateful to see the ruts smoothing out the uneven terrain and offering the ease and security of an established path. –BMT

" [Camping life] was indeed something new for us. The fixing of tents under the trees in the wood, the building of a campfire, the baking of our bread in baking kettles, the washing of our clothes and the tending of our baby boy just learning to walk were sometimes trying to one who had hardly ever cooked a meal, mixed bread or washed clothes. But, though some of the work was hard and many were the privations that we were beginning to feel, we still felt happy."[48]

Louise Charlotte Leuba Graehl
Age 31, Swiss convert, circa spring 1854, Robert L. Campbell company. Reminiscence, date uncertain.

" We saw a great many Gentile graves on the road. The cholera had slayed them terribly. There was wagons, tires, clothing, guns, bedding, boots and shoes scattered along the road."[49]

Elijah Averett
Age 39, summer 1851, Aaron Johnson company. Reminiscence, circa 1860s.

YOU ARE NEVER ALONE
John Burton
Ayres Natural Bridge, Wyoming
2016, oil on canvas

"There was wild weird romance about the country like some dream, some imaginary scene materialized. During the evenings the sound of music in different parts of the camp seems strangely harmonious with the almost deathlike solitude of those uninhabited regions."[50]

John Lingren
Age 18, Swedish convert, summer 1863, John F. Sanders company.
Reminiscence, 1893.

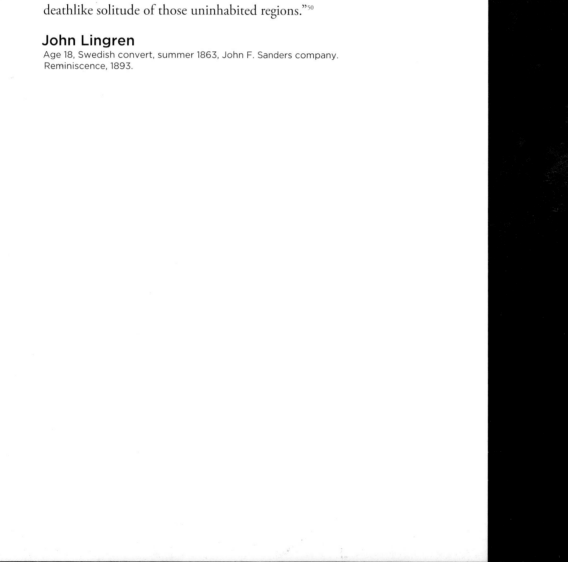

HIS PRESENCE WILL MY WANT SUPPLY

Josh Clare

Ayres Natural Bridge, Wyoming

2016, oil on canvas

" Passed an arch of stone which stretched entirely across the river and over hung by very high hills of red sand stone. The arch was more than 20 ft. high. Passing up the stream we found that it broke through the high mountain in a rough & rugged current. There were fresh signs of bear."[51]

Hosea Stout

Age 37, July 31, 1848, Brigham Young 1848 company. Trail journal.

John Burton

Near the Old Mormon Ferry, Casper, Wyoming

2015, oil on canvas

" I and Eliza Olivia [Stokes's daughter] traveled by the side of the Platte River a long way and in coming to a nice shallow creek which we had to cross, we pulled off our shoes and stockings and washed our feet and drank freely of the water."[52]

Henry Stokes

Age 33, English convert, August 30, 1862, Henry W. Miller company. Trail journal.

" On arriving at the North Platte and up the Sweetwater, not knowing how to take advantage of mountain travel, selecting feed ground, etc. my cattle died by drinking poisonous or alkali water. So much so that my team and many others was so reduced that we could not travel until aid was sent us from Salt Lake Valley by those who had emigrated the previous year."[53]

Robert Taylor Burton

Age 26, Canadian convert, summer 1848, Brigham Young 1848 company. Reminiscence, date uncertain.

ARTIST PERSPECTIVE One of the things I noticed while painting the trail was the long stretches where little clean water or wood seemed to be found. Such crucial life-sustaining resources would have been terribly missed. I can imagine how it must have felt after a long journey to find water. The idea of that desperate thirst reminded me of the scripture John 4:14: "But whosoever drinketh of the water that I shall give him shall never thirst; but the water that I shall give him shall be in him a well of water springing up into everlasting life." –JB

PRAISE YE HIS NAME

Josh Clare

Casper, Wyoming

2016, oil on canvas

"The sun was so hot that sometimes it seemed as if we could stand it no longer. Or sometimes the wind would blow the sand and dirt all over us. They told us in England that everyone had to eat a peck of dirt before he died. I had more than my peck while I was crossing the plains but it didn't take the place of food."[54]

Sarah Hancock Beesley

Age 19, English convert, summer 1859, George Rowley handcart company. Reminiscence, date uncertain.

THESE DEEDS SHALL THY MEMORIAL BE
Josh Clare

North Platte River, near the Old Mormon Ferry,
Casper, Wyoming

2016, oil on canvas

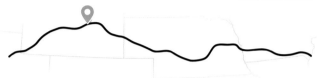

" Commenced crossing some waggons on a raft & some floated with poles under & by the side of them…. The poles broke under my waggon…and it turned up sidewise but 'twas righted & all got ashore without much injury. Some 12 or 15 waggons were got over during the day. A copious shower with hail fell about 3 o'clock…. The water is rising fast, & we concluded not to float any more waggons, as it is attended with much danger & risk."[55]

Norton Jacob

Age 42, June 14, 1847, Brigham Young 1847 pioneer company.
Trail journal.

HISTORICAL CONTEXT **NOT THE ONLY PIONEERS** The Mormon migration was part of a larger American experience. Mormons shared much of "their" trail with other pioneers who immigrated to Oregon and California during the mid-1800s. Actually, long portions of the Mormon route were primarily blazed by others.[56] But by improving the trail, the Saints made it easier for future immigrant companies, both Mormon and others, to travel west—thus warranting designation of the trail as the Mormon Trail. An example was at the last crossing of the North Platte River near present-day Casper, Wyoming. Mormons established a ferrying service open for hire by all westbound travelers.[57] –BCA

John Burton
Red Butte, Wyoming
2016, oil on canvas

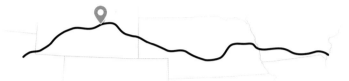

THE DISTANT LENS OF LAND-SCAPE A feeling of reverence is often evoked in the land, especially for those who see it as a scenic view, to be admired from a perch. Looking from afar allows the artist to be separate enough from the ruggedness to enjoy it as a type of picture. In this sense, the landscape acts as what art historian Lucy Lippard calls "a backdrop for the experience of viewing." She writes, "Like tourism, painting formalizes place into landscape."[58]

Yet for those like Norton Jacob and Thomas Bullock whose trail journals capture the mundane, the trail was not simply a site of isolated aesthetic enjoyment. Rather, it was a highway where large rocks and muddy roads that zigzagged with bad water framed their daily experience in tangible and ordinary ways. For them, it was not landscape but "place"—ordinary and even at times a trial. Yet from both experiences comes a sense of transcendence in the land. Through physical endurance, the trail offered Bullock and Jacob spiritual transformation as they acted on faith, and for Burton, the trail allowed him to bear witness to the grandeur of God's creation, to mark the history inherited in the land. -LAH

"Halt opposite 'Red Buttes' about 3/4 hour, no water— pretty good feed— hitch up— go half a mile & water cattle— then start … over gravel road— leaving a row of hills on the left— come to a natural wall— descend a gully— by zig zag, uneven road & very bad— turn to the right [and] halt in a hollow.… Bad water, saline deposit— scanty grass— no wood— but some Artemesia. I ascend [a] steep hill with Professor [Orson] Pratt [and] find some green & divers colored stones. Fine view of the country, it being a very steep high hill."[59]

Thomas Bullock
Age 30, English convert, June 19, 1847, Brigham Young pioneer company. Trail journal.

"This is a sterile barren region except low bottoms which afford good grass. But this is a place of most forbidding aspect, as one of my men expressed himself—'Such a country! Mire holes on the mountain, frost in July, salt water & no wood to cook with'— We had to resort to the buffalo chips again & sage brush to cook our meat."[60]

Norton Jacob
Age 42, June 19, 1847, Brigham Young 1847 pioneer company. Trail journal.

John Burton

Devil's Backbone and Rock Avenue, Wyoming

2016, oil on canvas

"Tarried [at] what is termed the Devil's Back Bone. It consists of a long range of rocks and looks as though they were thrown up from beneath and pointing upwards like ice in a jamb. It is a singular sight."[61]

Mary Elizabeth Rollins Lightner

Age 45, August 11, 1863, Alvus H. Patterson company. Trail journal.

"There is a high ridge of sharp pointed rocks running parallel with the road for near a quarter of a mile, leaving only sufficient space for wagons to pass. At the south point there is a very large rock [that] lays close to where the road makes a bend, making it somewhat difficult to get by without striking it. The road is also very rough with cobble stones.... This is considered by all to be the worst camping ground we have had on the journey…, the land being perfectly sandy and barren, and nothing growing but wild sage and a small prickly shrub something like the whins on the moors in Lancashire, England."[62]

William Clayton

Age 32, English convert, June 19, 1847, Brigham Young 1847 pioneer company. Trail journal.

ARTIST PERSPECTIVE As we traveled the trail over a four-year period, we tried to experience as many weather conditions as possible. This scene in Wyoming with an approaching lightning storm illustrates the type of exposure the Mormon pioneers would have encountered, with the large rock seemingly representing the words of Psalm 18:2: "The Lord is my rock, and my fortress, and my deliverer; my God, my strength, in whom I will trust; my buckler, and the horn of my salvation, and my high tower." For me, these rock formations appeared to offer a sense of protection and safety. –JB

HISTORICAL CONTEXT

PERPETUAL EMIGRATING FUND

Many of the Saints who carved their names into Independence Rock were beneficiaries of the church's Perpetual Emigrating Fund—a revolving loan program designed to assist Saints of modest means, especially European converts, in gathering to Zion. After 1850, numerous converts traveled in immigrant companies organized through the Perpetual Emigrating Fund. Church agents made all arrangements for travel across the Atlantic Ocean and riverboat or rail transport to trailheads that moved gradually westward over the years. Once fund recipients had settled in Utah, they were expected to reimburse the money so funds would be available for others to come to Zion.[63] –BCA

“Arose early, had breakfast soon, and all necessary arrangements made for visiting Independence Rock. Mounted its towering summit and viewed the surrounding objects, but I feel my pen or thoughts inadequate to the task of portraying a true picture of the awful grandeur and beauty of these scenes. Encamped about three miles this side of Devil's Gate.”[64]

Sarah Maria Mousley (Cannon)
Age 29, August 25, 1857, Jacob Hofheins company. Trail journal.

“We heard so much of Independence Rock long before we got there. They said we should have a dance on top of it, as we had many a dance while on the plains. We thought it would be so nice, but when got there, the company was so small that it was given up. We nooned at this place, but Father stayed long enough for us children to go all over it…. It is an immense rock with holes and crevices where the water is dripping cool and sparkling. We saw a great many names of persons that had been cut in the rock, but we were so disappointed in not having a dance.”[65]

Rachel Emma Woolley (Simmons)
Age 12, 1848, Brigham Young 1848 company. Reminiscence, circa 1881.

ROCK OF AGES

Josh Clare

Devil's Gate, Wyoming
2014, oil on canvas

" I was six or seven thousand miles from my native land, in a wild, rocky, mountain country, in a destitute condition, the ground covered with snow, the waters covered with ice, and I with three fatherless children with scarcely nothing to protect them from the merciless storms. When I retired to bed that night,…I had a stunning revelation. In my dream, my [deceased] husband stood by me and said— 'Cheer up, Elizabeth, deliverance is at hand.' The dream was fulfilled."[66]

Elizabeth Horrocks Jackson (Kingsford)

Age 30, English convert, October 1856, Edward Martin handcart company. Reminiscence, date uncertain.

ARTIST PERSPECTIVE Martin's Cove and Devil's Gate are very special places to me. There is an extremely sacred feeling there, a hallowed peace, as real as what I feel at the temple. I painted there on the last day of my trip in February 2012. To do a small color sketch in the quiet of a snowy day, alone with no sound but the gentle trickle of the Sweetwater River while the sun set on Devil's Gate, was an experience I'll never forget. –JC

" Devil's Gate Rock is two perpendicular walls found by measurement to be four hundred feet above the river, which runs through a chasm one thousand feet in length, and one hundred thirty feet in breadth. In this chasm the water tumbles and foams with the noise of a cataract over massive fragments of rock which have fallen from above."[67]

John Lingren
Age 18, Swedish convert, summer 1863, John F. Sanders company. Reminiscence, 1893.

" Stopped … near … the Devil's Gate. The river here has forced a channel through a mountain whose perpendicular rocks rise 400 feet & just wide enough for the river to run…. Some boys have ascend[ed] to the top by a rugged path & were seen from below with their feet hanging over the giddy precipice careless of danger and dropping stones into the abyss below, counting the seconds which each took in its fall. This was foolhardy but boys will be boys."[68]

Lorenzo Brown
Age 25, August 11, 1848, Brigham Young 1848 company. Reminiscence, circa 1856.

ARTIST PERSPECTIVE
I first arrived at Devil's Gate alone in the early evening. In the silence of the chilly, windless air, I watched the warm evening light rake across this natural wonder. As the orange of the sky faded into the blue of night, I thought of my ancestors who passed this way and of how quickly the complexity of their lives, their experiences, and their stories had come and then passed. –BMT

LOOKING WEST

Bryan Mark Taylor

Devil's Gate, Wyoming

2014, oil on canvas

" We have been for some days passing 'the Rocky Mountains.' They are rather more wonderful than beautiful—yet they are certainly sublime. It seems something marvelous & mysterious that our cavalcade should pass along breaking the eternal silence of these wild places. My feelings are undefinable but there is a degree of awe & sadness about them to me."[69]

Hannah Tapfield King

Age 46, English convert, August 28, 1853, Claudius V. Spencer company. Reminiscence, circa 1864–1872.

HISTORICAL CONTEXT

HANDCART COMPANIES From 1856 to 1860, Mormons organized ten handcart companies. Most succeeded. Two companies—the Edward Martin and James G. Willie companies—started too late in the season in 1856 and had to be rescued from autumn snows in Wyoming. These handcart stories have come to dominate popular perceptions regarding the pioneers and the Mormon Trail. In reality, over 95 percent of all Mormon pioneers traveled in wagon trains. Fewer than 5 percent were handcart pioneers.[70] –BCA

I CAN'T BUT I WILL (THE SWEETWATER)
John Burton
Martin's Cove, Wyoming
2016, oil on canvas

" The time came when we were all too tired to move, so we huddled in our covers, close to each other for warmth. It was snowing and we were so tired. Suddenly we heard a shout, and through the swirling snow we saw men, wagons and mules coming toward us. Slowly we realized that help had come. The wagons brought food and clothing. They hauled in wood for us and as we gathered around the huge fire and ate the delicious morsels of food, we came alive enough to thank the Lord for his mercy to us."[71]

Sarah James
Age 19, English convert, October 1856, James G. Willie handcart company. Reminiscence, date uncertain.

" We were caught in a heavy snowstorm on the Sweetwater, and the last of our flour was gone. The captain called us together, and said that all the provisions were gone, except some few crackers which he had saved for the sick and the small children.... Many died from the effect of want and cold, I myself have helped to bury...ten to fifteen in a single day.... We used to boil the bones [of cattle] and drink the soup and eat what little meat there was. We greedily devoured the hides also. I myself took a piece of hide when I could get it, scorched off the hair on the fire, roasted it a little on the coals, cut it in little pieces so that I could swallow it and bolted it down my throat for supper and thought it was most delicious."[72]

George Cunningham
Age 16, Scottish convert, October 1856, James G. Willie handcart company. Reminiscence, 1876.

EVENING AT THE SWEETWATER

Bryan Mark Taylor

Near Third Crossing of the
Sweetwater River, Wyoming

2016, oil on canvas

ARTIST PERSPECTIVE

Evening at the Sweetwater depicts the slow meandering beauty of the river, creating a peaceful scene. In contrast to the serenity of the water, the sparse landscape and deep tones of the setting sun give the landscape a sense of foreboding. There isn't much civilization in this remote corner of the world, so by necessity we set up camp. Finding myself amid such isolation, I imagined the nighttime must have sparked similar feelings for the travelers—a time for rest and relief, but also caution and concern. –BMT

" We traveled … on the banks of the river, then halted for noon as the road and the river separated. The road very sandy…. We continued our journey and after traveling 6¾ mi[les] we [again] came to the banks of the river…. There is plenty of grass on the river banks but no wood…. The Sweetwater Mountains appear very plain from here and all the mountains that are in sight are all covered with snow."[73]

Howard Egan
Age 32, Irish convert, June 23, 1847, Brigham Young pioneer company. Trail journal.

" Every day wafts us so much farther from the land of our birth and home of our parents. The idea frequently causes a deep drawn sigh to escape me and almost every morning I find my spirit has been wandering back to the scenes of my childhood and youth, and mingling with the companions of my early days, but oh! Those days are past never more to return."[74]

Caroline Barnes Crosby
Age 41, September 22, 1848, Willard Richards company. Trail journal.

KNOWN, UNKNOWN PLACES In Taylor's *Evening at the Sweetwater* (page 89), the cool water in the foreground reflects the dusk sky in the background. The view of the land is clearly drawing upon nineteenth-century Romanticism as the Sweetwater River, as seen from Taylor's eye, is idealized as much as it is illuminated. For Caroline Barnes Crosby, the land she saw along the trek west was foreign to her and was distinctly different than and miles away from her known homeland. By contrast, painting the Sweetwater allowed Taylor to mark and pay tribute to one of the most well-known (and revered) places along the Mormon Pioneer Trail. In the words of artist Marlene Creates, "The land is important to me, but even more important is the idea that it becomes a 'place' because someone has been there."[75]

While Taylor camped along the banks of the river to capture the best light, it was not only a picturesque site for him but also a place rooted in people gone before. Grounded in memories and stories that attest to the legacy of faith he inherited, the viewing of it brought him closer to home, not further away. Said art historian Lucy Lippard, "If we have seen a place through many years, each view, no matter how banal, is a palimpsest."[76] The word *palimpsest* makes reference to ancient manuscripts that were scraped and then reused. Through this process, the paper bore the ghosts of previous writings; traces of what was written upon the paper held the imprint of the past. For Lippard, Creates, and Taylor, the land is not a neutral, foreign place as it was for Crosby; rather, it is laden with meaning and history and is imprinted with the stories of the past. –LAH

CROSSING THE SWEETWATER
Bryan Mark Taylor
Sweetwater Crossing, Jeffrey City, Wyoming
2014, oil on canvas

" Came to the Sweetwater where there was an abundance of most beautiful fish. We took a net … [and] stopped the train and began fishing. Caught fish sufficient for three hearty meals for the entire camp."[77]

Sarah Maria Mousley (Cannon)
Age 29, August 29, 1857, Jacob Hofheins company. Trail journal.

" As we traveled along the Sweetwater River … we traveled over bad roads of sand, mud and rocks. So bad was the roads that we could not make much headway."[78]

Sarah DeArmon Pea Rich
Age 32, September 1, 1847, Charles C. Rich company. Reminiscence, circa 1890–1893.

PROMISES AND POLLYWOGS
John Burton

Fremont County, Wyoming

2015, oil on canvas

"I used to see other children running along barefooted, and thought it would be nice to take my shoes off too. But my feet were not accustomed to such rough usage, and I was generally glad to put them on again.... Another favorite pastime consisted of walking far enough ahead of the train to get a little time to play; when we would drive the huge crickets ... and build corrals of sand or rocks to put them in, calling them our cattle. Another inducement to keep ahead of the waggons, was our fear of riding across the creeks and bad places in the road, as the waggons were sometimes upset. In keeping ahead we managed to get across if possible before the teams came up. If the rivers were not too deep we pulled off our shoes and stockings and waded through."[79]

Mary Jane Mount (Tanner)
Age 10, summer 1847, Abraham O. Smoot–George B. Wallace company. Reminiscence, circa 1872–1884.

THIS TOO SHALL PASS

Bryan Mark Taylor

Rocky Ridge, Wyoming

2015, oil on canvas

" We had our first experience at sleeping in the great outdoors—a rather terrifying one until we got used to it. Every single night, it seemed to me, it stormed. The inky darkness would be broken by sudden, blinding flashes of lightning, and the steady howl of the storm by roars of rolling thunder. The seven of us huddled even closer together, but not even tent walls and bed clothes could shut out the blinding flashes of terrific claps of thunder."[80]

Amelia Eliza Slade (Bennion)
Age 9, English convert, August 1864, Warren S. Snow company.
Reminiscence, date uncertain.

ARTIST PERSPECTIVE This painting depicts the often dark and foreboding horizon along the trail. The power and fury of storms must have struck terror in the minds of all travelers and made progress difficult, if not impossible, for a time. The rich, dark blues and greens of this scene contrast the warm, light-filled hope of the unseen sun above. –BMT

HALLOWED GROUND
Bryan Mark Taylor
Rock Creek Hollow, Wyoming
2014, oil on canvas

❝ I took a walk by myself. Passed through some of the most singular looking places I ever saw; it seemed to me that nature in her playful moments had formed curiosities for her own sport.❞[81]

Caroline Barnes Crosby
Age 41, August 4, 1848, Willard Richards company. Trail journal.

ARTIST PERSPECTIVE Rock Creek Hollow felt like a small oasis in a barren and generally inhospitable area of the trail. The big clouds and the distant spine of the Wind River Mountains to the north were softened by a shaft of light illuminating a part of the valley. I felt tragedy redeemed by beauty in this solemn and sacred place. –BMT

LIGHT OF LIFE

Josh Clare

Fremont County, Wyoming

2016, oil on canvas

" The scenery [is] grand and terrible. I have walked under overhanging rocks which seemed only to need the pressure of a finger to send them down headlong. Many of them resemble the ruins of old castles, and it needs but a little stretch of the imagination to fancy yourself in the deserted hall of a palace or of a temple."[82]

Jean Rio Griffiths Baker

Age 41, English convert, August 29, 1851, John Brown company.
Trail journal.

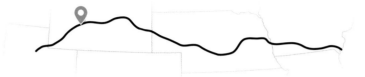

HISTORICAL CONTEXT

CUMBERLAND GAP OF THE WEST

Crossing South Pass was not as dramatic as some pioneers may have anticipated. It was not a hole or breach in a mountainous landscape. Rather, the pass was an almost imperceptible ascent across open terrain over the Continental Divide. It was the one route through the Rockies that was tame enough to accommodate nineteenth-century wagon trains. Altitude at the pass is over seven thousand feet,[83] so it was common for pioneers to encounter cold weather there, particularly companies who traveled through later in the year. Approaching South Pass in early October 1849, a company led by George A. Smith hunkered down for several days during a snowstorm that made travel difficult and dangerous. George's wife Bathsheba Bigler Smith recorded: "It was very grievous to hear the children cry, the ox low, the cow bawl, the sheep bleat, the pig squeal, the duck quack, [and the] chicken cheep, and we couldn't tell them the cause why they had to suffer thus."[84] –BCA

"Ten miles brought us to the south pass. The ascent is quite gradual, so much so that hardly any knew he was going up hill. Altitude of pass 7085 feet. The descent on the west side is more abrupt but still gradual."[85]

Lorenzo Brown
Age 25, September 3, 1848, Brigham Young company. Reminiscence, circa 1856.

"The road [has been] pretty good the last few days. Prospect wild. Were it not for the lovely skies and pure atmosphere it would be bleak indeed, but they are something heavenly!—different to anything we ever saw in England—reminding me of Byron's exclamation, 'So cloudless clear, & purely beautiful, that God alone was to be seen in Heaven!'"[86]

Hannah Tapfield King
Age 46, English convert, September 1853, Claudius V. Spencer company. Reminiscence, circa 1864–1872.

❝Weather cold, cloudy & wet. Heavy wind & rain most of the night. The wolves howl at night so bad that one sometimes can but think that he is in sectarian purgatory.... The wolves took one of Father [Reynolds] Cahoon's boots from under his wagon & carried it about 1/2 mile where it was accidentally found."[87]

Lorenzo Brown
Age 25, September 1, 1848, Brigham Young 1848 company. Reminiscence, circa 1856.

❝Loose fragments of rocks made it very bad travelling.... The weather grew cooler towards evening, some large clouds rising in the west which favored the teams considerably.... During the day [we traveled] 23¾ [miles], which is the greatest day's journey we have made since leaving Winter Quarters. The camp was formed by moonlight. There seems to be plenty of feed for teams but no wood for fuel."[88]

William Clayton
Age 32, English convert, June 29, 1847, Brigham Young pioneer company. Trail journal.

CURATOR'S RESPONSE

KANT AND THE SUBLIME The German philosopher Immanuel Kant remains one of the leading figures who shaped the discourse on the sublime, primarily through two texts, *Observations on the Feeling of the Beautiful and Sublime* (1764) and *Critique of Judgment* (1790). According to scholar Thomas Weiskel, one of the sources of the sublime as described by Kant is to create a feeling of infinity, even if the experience of infinity is just perceived as such and is in reality artificial.[89] Weiskel writes, "The feeling is one of *on and on*, of being lost.... The imagery appropriate to this variety of the sublime is usually characterized by featureless (meaningless) horizontality."[90] Clare's *Benediction* blurs the foreground, removing clear landmarks and geographic features by which to orient oneself. The land is simply open, a blank and empty canvas that seems to go on forever. –LAH

John Burton
Near Church Butte, Wyoming
2016, oil on canvas

MORMON PIONEER DISTINCTIVE-NESS Mormons experienced many things common to all western pioneers. At the same time, most concede that the Saints' experience was also distinctive in important ways. For example, Mormons migrated collectively as families organized into companies and subcompanies of hundreds, fifties, and tens—"villages on wheels"—led by men appointed from among themselves. Most important, the bedrock of Mormon motivation was faith in revealed commandments to establish Zion—God's kingdom on earth preparatory to Jesus Christ's second coming. The religious nature of their enterprise distinctively shaped and tempered their frontier pioneering experience and set them apart from most other American pioneers.[91] –BCA

" Our minds were so much delighted with the novelty of the surrounding scenery that we almost forgot we were a little past the meridian of life, and for a moment imagined ourselves mere children, sporting at leisure. All the animal we saw was one little rabbit which ran from us in great fear and a few very pretty birds that seemed [to] make homes in the old cedar trees."[92]

Caroline Barnes Crosby
Age 41, August 11, 1848, Willard Richards company. Trail journal.

CARRY ON
Josh Clare
Muddy Creek Camp, Wyoming
2016, oil on canvas

"At Fort Bridger … to my great joy, I was able to purchase forty pounds of very fine, fresh beef. I never saw finer in the London markets, and that is saying a good deal…. The beef was only ten cents per pound. Travelled on until we came to Muddy Fork and encamped."[93]

Jean Rio Griffiths Baker
Age 41, English convert, September 19, 1851, John Brown company. Trail journal.

SONGS OF GLORY

Josh Clare

Near Bear River Crossing, Wyoming

2016, oil on canvas

"The grandeur of nature filled me with grateful aspirations. The beautiful camping grounds, which were so clean, that one was led to conclude no human foot had ever trodden there. So green was the grass, so delightful the wild flowers, so umbrageous the grounds on the banks of the rivers!"[94]

Louisa Barnes Pratt
Age 45, summer 1848, Brigham Young 1848 company.
Reminiscence, 1850–1880.

"Yesterday we travelled till quite late & passed some splendid bluffs ruins. These bluffs are something I cannot describe. They are sublime & mysterious— There is beauty & order in them, and it requires no very fanciful stretch of imagination to form baronial buildings—'Keeps'— gateways…. They are very high— I should like to hear a philosophical description of them— They please and interest me more than [I] have language to express— There is much design in them—yet they say they are solely the work of Nature— Well I must leave them like all mysterious things."[95]

Hannah Tapfield King
Age 46, English convert, September 10, 1853, Claudius V. Spencer company. Reminiscence, circa 1864–1872.

"We have passed beautiful & sublime scenery, Echo Canyon especially—that surpasses anything I have yet seen before—And some spots yesterday I felt I could live and die in!… Beautiful bluffs, beautiful canyons & some things that were anything but beautiful—sorrows & troubles & tears! etc. etc. were mixed up with the beauties of nature."[96]

Hannah Tapfield King
Age 46, English convert, September 1853, Claudius V. Spencer company. Reminiscence, circa 1864–1872.

ARTIST PERSPECTIVE As we traveled the footsteps of the pioneers, there was nowhere more idyllic than Echo Canyon, with its towering red cliffs and a cool stream lined with cottonwood trees. I could never capture the splendor of this spot with paint on canvas because its beauty was too magnificent. Echo Canyon is one of the first locations on the trail in the state of Utah, and immediately the pioneers must have felt something special about the landscape. –JB

"Scenery was varied and changeable. Many curious looking rocks of different shapes and forms were seen on the right hand side of us and on the left hand of the road were to be seen mountains covered with brush and grass while the rocks were adorned with pine trees growing in abundance in all kinds of places where a person would be supposed to think there would be no nourishment. The creek ran down about the middle of the canyon, and in some places it made the road very narrow. On both sides of [the] creek willows grew in great abundance. Their leaves now indicated the season of the year. They were turned to a beautiful orange yellow color."[97]

Henry Stokes
Age 33, English convert, October 13, 1862, Henry W. Miller company. Trail journal.

CHANGING SEASONS
Bryan Mark Taylor
Echo Canyon, Utah
2014, oil on canvas

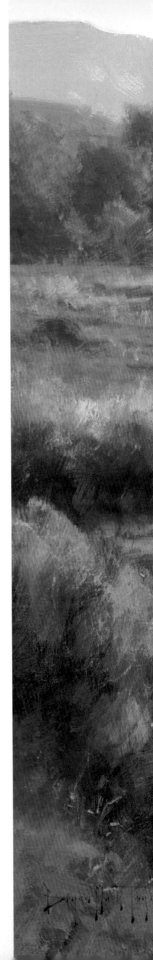

" I well remember that when we camped in Echo Canyon that Sister [Sarah] Squires was confined in the morning. She had a lovely baby girl and they named her Echo. The morning she was born the father was running around camp enquiring of everybody if they had a pin to give him to pin something around the baby, but I don't think that he was able to get one. The brethren fixed the wagon very warm and comfortable for Sister Squires and both her and baby arrived safe into the city."[98]

Patience Loader (Rozsa Archer)
Age 29, English convert, October 1856, Edward Martin handcart company. Reminiscence, circa 1890.

" We camped at the mouth of Echo Canyon on the Weber River, at a small town, Henefer, which was named after the only people living there at that time. Mr. Henefer donated five bushels of potatoes if we would dig them. Fishing was good in the Weber River, and so after the potatoes were dug and the fish caught and cooked, of course, everyone had a treat."[99]

Daniel Robison
Age 29, summer 1860, Daniel Robison handcart company. Reminiscence, date uncertain.

112

John Burton
Big Mountain, Utah
2016, oil on canvas

"Our road led us over a very high mountain…. Our position commanded a fine view of the country;… and in the distance could be seen a hollow, it seemed little more, which we were told was the valley of the Great Salt Lake, and our future destination. How many weary feet have stood on that mountain since and tried to look into the valley, wondering what it held for them. I believe, with us, the one thought was rest, and thankfulness that our journey was nearly over. I wonder as we near the end our life's journey if we shall gaze into the valley of peace and feel to rejoice that we are nearly there?"[100]

Mary Jane Mount (Tanner)
Age 10, autumn 1847, Abraham O. Smoot–George B. Wallace company. Reminiscence, circa 1872–1884.

"We ascended and descended a very high mountain. The teams had all they could do to draw the loads. On arriving at the top we had a glimpse of the valley of Salt Lake which we had so long been striving to reach. We all rejoiced and thought we were the same as there, but when we came to descend the mountain we found we had one of the worst and most crooked roads to pass over that ever was seen. We however got through safely."[101]

Caroline Barnes Crosby
Age 41, October 10, 1848, Willard Richards company. Trail journal.

"We came to what is called Big Mountain, and it is rightly named. We had to double teams to get up, that is, take all the teams in camp and put them all on two or three wagons, take them up to the top, then come back for others…. Then coming down put them on the back of the wagons to hold them back. Those that came when we did know something of the difficulties of traveling. Five months of that kind gets monotonous, after awhile, but we were near our journey's end … [and] could rejoice even withal."[102]

Rachel Emma Woolley (Simmons)
Age 12, 1848, Brigham Young 1848 company. Reminiscence, circa 1881.

" Of all the splendid scenery, and awful roads, that have ever been since creation, I think this day's journey has beaten them all. We had encamped last night at the foot of a mountain which we had to ascend this morning. This was hard enough on our poor worn-out animals, but the road after was completely covered with stones, as large as bushel boxes, stumps of trees, with here and there mudholes in which our poor oxen sunk to the knees.... [But] the grandeur of the scenery, to my mind, takes away all fear."[103]

Jean Rio Griffiths Baker
Age 41, English convert, September 28, 1851, John Brown company. Trail journal.

" As we gazed down the yawning chasm that lay before us; the narrow road with rocks and bushes on each side, and leading, we could not see where, was a sight to make the strongest heart falter. My mother felt that she was not equal to the task of guiding her oxen down that fearful road, and my father tried to get a man to drive the team down for her. They were all fully occupied with their own teams, and she had to go down the best she could, hanging to the horns of her cattle, and leaving her dress as usual on the bushes to mark her way. I wonder if those coming after knew what those tattered rags meant."[104]

Mary Jane Mount (Tanner)
Age 10, autumn 1847, Abraham O. Smoot-George B. Wallace company. Reminiscence, circa 1872–1884.

John Burton

Emigration Canyon, Utah

2016, oil on canvas

HARDEST PART FOR LAST After traveling hundreds of weary miles, many Saints were disheartened near the end of their journey to encounter the worst mountain passes on the Mormon Trail. To reach the Salt Lake Valley, they struggled through the Wasatch Range, following the so-called Hastings Cutoff that the ill-fated California-bound Donner–Reed party had pioneered in 1846.[105] (The effort slowed the party, which contributed to them later becoming snowbound in the high Sierras, with fatal consequences.) Regarding this last segment of the trail, historian Richard E. Bennett writes, "Hauling wagon trains through dense willow underbrush, up steep climbs, and down precipitous, life-threatening descents was surely the challenge of the entire trek."[106]

In 1850, Parley P. Pratt opened an alternative toll route—the Golden Pass Road—that entered the Salt Lake Valley through Parley's Canyon rather than Emigration Canyon.[107] After 1862, this became the preferred route for most immigrants. It was still challenging, however. Henry Stokes found it "difficult to pass through" and "very wearisome and dangerous. Brethren walked by side of wagons on the upper side and held on to the side of the wagon to prevent it from capsizing or tipping over."[108] –BCA

❝As we neared our destination, our journey became wearisome and full of toil. Grass became scarce, cattle began to give out, often, when an ox gave out, a cow was put in its place. The roads were rough, wagons had to be pitched up, till sometimes you would wonder how they could go at all. One of my calamities was my lock-chain giving out, and in going down a hill I had to hold the nigh ox by the horn and tap the off one over the face and keep saying, 'Whoa, Back; Whoa, Back,' and nearly hold my breath till I got down to the bottom, then stop, draw a breath of relief, see that all was right, then on again, for others were right on our heels and we had to get out of their way, (you can just imagine what a condition our skirts were in.)."[109]

Ann Agatha Walker Pratt

Age 18, English convert, September 1847, Daniel Spencer–Perrigrine Sessions company. Reminiscence, circa 1893.

❝The mountains on both sides were so very high and the ravines so crooked that we could not see but a short distance and it looked as though we were shut up in a gulch without any chance for escape. The ground was quite rising for about five miles.… After we got to the top of the hill we had a long, steep hill to go down."[110]

Levi Jackman

Age 49, July 20, 1847, Brigham Young 1847 pioneer company. Trail journal.

"I never shall forget the last day we traveled, and arrived in the Valley…. When my eyes rested on the beautiful entrancing sight—the Valley; Oh! how my heart swelled within me, I could have laughed and cried, such a comingling of emotions I cannot describe. My soul was filled with thankfulness to God for bringing us to a place of rest and safety—a home. No doubt our valley looks astonishingly beautiful to the strangers who come here now, but it cannot evoke the same emotions as it did to us, poor weary tired, worn out, ragged travelers. When I drove into camp, unyoked my cattle, and sat down on the wagon tongue, and began to realize that, in the morning I would not have to hitch up and toil through another day, such a feeling of rest—blessed rest—permeated my whole being that is impossible to describe, and cannot be realized except by those who have passed through similar scenes."[111]

Ann Agatha Walker Pratt
Age 18, English convert, September 28, 1847, Daniel Spencer-Perrigrine Sessions company. Reminiscence, circa 1893.

"As we enter the valley of the mountains and look out over the vast land of Zion, I am dismayed by the very immensity of the view. The boundless silence, and to see miles of sage brush everywhere. Behind us now are the heart aches and many thousands of silent tears that fell on the long unknown trail. I remember my dear home in England, of the flowers and trees and beautiful surroundings at that safe home. And I am home sick for my dear mother and father. But just as I have covered those endless hundreds of miles, so now I will begin work with renewed faith, begin the task of building a good home in this new wilderness."[112]

Mary Pugh Scott
Age 26, English convert, circa August 1848, Heber C. Kimball company. Reminiscence, 1877.

INTERVIEW WITH ARTISTS

John Burton, Josh Clare, and Bryan Mark Taylor
by Laura Allred Hurtado

LAURA: Let's start with the concept. Why did you decide to do this project?

JOHN: I converted to The Church of Jesus Christ of Latter-day Saints about ten years ago, although both my mother and father have pioneer ancestors. I was always intrigued by the incredible hardships Mormon pioneers experienced because of their faith, and their history always seemed to beckon me to learn more about the church. A few years after my baptism, I met Bryan, and I felt impressed that we needed to do an art exhibition about the pioneer trail. He introduced me to Josh, and the project really felt inspired, even from the very beginning.

LAURA: *Saints at Devil's Gate* is an interesting title, partly because it brings to mind a specific company of pioneers—who aren't represented in the paintings—and partly because it references an exact location, although the exhibition depicts most of the length of the trail.

JOHN: For me, the title has two meanings. Devil's Gate, Wyoming, is the location where the Martin handcart company experienced great difficulties—freezing weather, exhaustion, and starvation. Yet in these deprivations, they were not forgotten by the Lord or their fellow Saints, and the story of their suffering has made this area an iconic and sacred spot.

The second meaning, for me, is a metaphorical one. While the pioneers faced extreme physical difficulty, which required great fortitude to overcome, today as Latter-day Saints we continue to struggle and seek to manifest and maintain our faith in the face of multiple trials. Like the Willie and Martin handcart companies, I believe we are not forgotten but have an opportunity to be rescued as well. So the title doesn't reflect tragedy but triumph. As Mormon painters, it was important that we took the time to stand witness of the suffering of the pioneers and to use their stories as a source of strength in our own lives.

BRYAN: Right. Some of the most memorable and well-known stories of the Mormon Trail come from the journal entries of these two companies, and in some ways it's the

Bryan Mark Taylor's ancestor John Watkins was the company bugler for the Edward Martin company at the age of twenty-two.

initial reason that drew us to the project. John, Josh, and I have ancestors who were either rescued or were rescuers, so the story is personal in that regard.

LAURA: In fact, so do I. My ancestor Redick Allred was a rescuer. Also, it's a well-known story that sometimes overshadows those of all the other Mormon overland companies that traveled safely over a period of more than twenty years.

BRYAN: Right. For us, the title embodies historical, spiritual, and aesthetic realities, but it also has some ambiguity as it relates to the project and invites viewers to make their own connection. It can function as a literal reference to the Saints in a particular time on a particular part of the Mormon Trail or, more important, as a metaphor of good people past and present, here or there, trying to handle life's difficulties. It is also an invitation to find goodness and beauty even in the most tumultuous times. It suggests there is a spiritual and human narrative in the midst of formidable and often deserted landscapes, and the exhibition, I believe, makes an attempt to more broadly embody the greater story of the western migration.

LAURA: Why modern landscapes with historical quotations?

JOSH: The basic premise of the show from the start was to paint the trail as it appears today and to give people an opportunity to remember the deep faith of those who sacrificed much to come start life over in the desert. That could be done with historical work, but painting the trail as it is today felt more honest, more natural. It's certainly subtler, and because of that, the paintings rely pretty heavily upon titles, journal entries, and pioneer reminiscences to tell the story.

LAURA: That makes sense. It's more subtle in terms of messaging because if you look at the paintings without knowing the story of what happened there, they are just landscapes. Additionally, while there are some well-known pioneer artists, I can't think of any grand landscape paintings done on-site, at least not to the scale of the exhibition. So in a sense, there isn't a historical document that could constitute a show of this scale. Certainly C. C. A. Christensen, George M. Ottinger, Peter Olsen Hansen (in Heber C. Kimball's journal), and Frederick Piercy painted or sketched the trail.[1] In fact, we have one of the earliest known paintings by Christensen, which depicts the company he was in. But still, these examples are exceptions, not the rule.

Inside cover of Heber C. Kimball journal with drawings by his scribe Peter Olsen Hansen.

BRYAN: Like Josh said, we wanted to document how the trail looks today in contrast to the feelings and experiences of the Mormon pioneers. Some areas of the trail have been left unchanged, while other areas have become cities. By avoiding any theatrical or historical drama, I believe we can get a better understanding of the reality of these places and appreciate how the pioneers thought and felt about their trek west.

LAURA: Bryan, can you expand on that? What do you mean by "theatrical or historical drama"?

BRYAN: It's like a documentary versus a historical epic. The goal of an epic film is to re-create the past, but it also glamorizes and dramatizes it; whereas, in a documentary, although subjectivity still exists, the goal is to experience the past in a way that is much more natural, much more real. So I think what we were trying to do instead of dressing people up, staging historical scenes, and making paintings from those re-creations, which certainly have their place, was to just show the viewer how the pioneers might have experienced the land and the trail by the way we have experienced it. In some ways, I think we get closer to the truth of what happened than a theatrical painting because we are trying to see and experience it in a more of a direct medium—painting the actual locations and the actual weather conditions instead of trying to stage it.

LAURA: I like the idea that figurative paintings have a performative element to them—a staging. Youth conference treks have a similar reenacting element to them. There are costumes—teenagers dressed in bonnets, collarless shirts, vests, and aprons. It's not just limited to treks, though. It's celebrating Pioneer Day in a stake center parking lot, or a baseball field in Los Angeles. Mormons love the reenactment. And you're right that there is something to be learned from that experience, from the reenactment. But there is also something quite powerful, even for those on a trek, to see the land, at least in segments, not far altered from how the pioneers experienced it.

And yet, there is certainly the reality of a place and then there's the lens, or frame, or crop that an artist takes. So

how do you respond to that idea of the crop that an artist makes in relationship to the idea that these pieces of art take a documentary approach?

Pioneer reenactment has long been a part of Mormon culture. Pioneer Day celebration, Palos Verdes Stake, California, July 23, 1984. Rolling Hills High School baseball field. Curator, age four.

BRYAN: Yes, that is certainly true. There is a filter that goes through the mind of an artist. However, I think there is less of that filtering process because you don't have to add other theatrical elements to it. It's just you and the landscape. So it is a little bit more of a direct or closer way to access the space, the experience. I guess that part of it is raw contact between you and the landscape. It's not scripted. The paintings depict how we found the weather to be when we arrived. So, in that sense, it's truer. That's not to say that we didn't change a few things—we did. But I think there is a lot less in terms of what needed to be changed. So the filter is not as thick in my opinion. There is a little more of a raw quality to it, and I think that is what is really attractive about a documentary that you don't find in a drama.

LAURA: Because, in drama, what you find problematic is that there is a forced narrative or even a singular narrative. Is that right?

BRYAN: Yes. Exactly. A narrative. Documentaries also tell narrative stories, but they are more fact based or journalistic. I think that more transparent quality is something that contemporary minds demand a little more of than before. We want to step outside of the script and look behind the frame a little bit. We want to look behind at the inner workings. I think that's what this show accomplishes. It just shows the land. Yes, the land is at times framed, cropped, and artistically rendered, but there is an honesty there.

Some of the paintings show just that. Some of them show very mundane areas, so instead of trying to make the narrative or the viewer's experience really sweet or really heart wrenching, we just show the land.

LAURA: But in some ways your paintings create a mood that certainly evokes a feeling. I think you're right that the sense of what it evokes is also in part what the viewer brings to it. So if the viewer doesn't know anything about the Mormon pioneers and sees a painting of the Sweetwater River, Martin's Cove, or Mount Pisgah, it doesn't mean the same thing unless the viewer himself or herself has given that place significance—unless the viewer can, in effect, see the ghosts that are there. So I think that's where the subtlety is.

JOSH: I think it's a useful metaphor that Bryan is using regarding a theatrical movie, which can sometimes be about making a record of someone else's experience versus really trying to make a record of your own experience. It's a nice way to talk about what the show is about. In a lot of ways, it was just us out there in the landscape, feeling the landscape the way it is.

LAURA: That's right. And paired with the trail journals and reminiscences there is a narrative created, but it isn't singular. In part, it is fragmented from the overall context, but there are multiple perspectives offered. Certainly, the perspective of the artist is offered, but also the writing and reflections of multiple pioneers. For me, this pairing adds nuance to a place and the types of experiences one can have in that specific place. I also think you are referencing the idea that viewers can sometimes tell when an artwork's message is a little too heavy handed, a little too didactic, or a little too message driven, and that heavy-handedness can sometimes make it more difficult for viewers to feel a personal connection to the work because they stumble over the weight of the message, which, being spoon-fed, doesn't allow for real engagement or variance of perspective.

JOHN: For us, this show really invites the viewer to be part of the experience. The viewer is invited into the landscape and can witness it in some of the same ways the pioneers did. This land looks peaceful, safe, beautiful, or dangerous. Without anything filtering you from the landscape, you're viewing it like the pioneers viewed it.

LAURA: Without the filter of a dramatic narrative on top, yes. Certainly there is still subjectivity, but it's subtle; the message is subtle. Part of this project feels very much like a pilgrimage. There is this sense of paying tribute. You are walking where they walked. You are walking on holy land. It is quite different from a reenactment, but it is still a type of looking at the land through a historical filter. I was wondering if you could respond to that.

Photograph of John Burton's easel and plein air painting (Council Bluffs, Iowa, 2014).

JOSH: For us it was really personal, and it did feel like a pioneer trek to me, although I've never gone on one myself. Through the process of painting the trail, I was trying hard to remember the pioneers. But for people who view the paintings, I think the experience is subtler. I'm hoping that the viewers will get that sense of ancestors and of the Mormon pioneers. But it still is a quiet way to remember them; it's a subtle way because we're not hitting them over the head with handcarts and oxen. It's really just a river. But for us, it was a pilgrimage.

JOHN: The idea of the show—it's really more of a whisper. We don't have big oxen or covered wagons. We don't have things that are going to be screaming at the viewer. It's a much quieter show. As the viewers walk around, we are really asking them to participate.

BRYAN: This is not a reenactment in my view. The land is still very raw and still very open, and it's still a big part of the American story today. So, in part, what we wanted to depict was what the trail looked like at the beginning of the twenty-first century. And I think as we look back at this project, it will also be its own history. In that sense, the trail becomes new and fresh and kind of alive instead of digging up old bones. We are trying to give it a fresh look and vibrancy.

LAURA: I do think it has a lot of freshness to it, and the work is consistently strong. And yet you draw upon a nineteenth-century art tradition of landscape.

BRYAN: You know, a lot of it could be just like the sculptors and the artists of the past. You see the sculpture of David being redone in various periods, and it reflects not only the story of the Bible but also the society that the artists lived in. So that's what we are trying to do as well.

LAURA: Michelangelo's *David* depicts a biblical story in an Italian Renaissance style that draws strongly upon traditions developed by Greco-Roman artistic practices. For that example, absolutely, there is looking to the old and making it contemporary to the artist's time, and I think there are similar stylistic elements of that within your project as well. I'm interested in the idea that the artistic styles that you are using are very nineteenth century. The sketches are done on-site, en plein air. Can we talk about the use of landscape painting to tell this story?

JOHN: Stylistically I was really influenced by Russian Impressionism.

BRYAN: In response to the influence of nineteenth-century landscape painting, there is certainly a tradition that all of us have studied as artists. But going back to

the subject of David, Michelangelo depicted him, and then later Bernini depicted him quite differently. Both artists were sculptors, but Michelangelo's work reflects the context of the Italian Renaissance and Bernini, the Baroque. So although both studied the classical traditions, because of their time and place, they selected different things, and they came up with different results because of it. So here we are, 170 years or so after the pioneers passed through the Mormon Trail. Not only does the landscape in parts look a bit different, but we also transform it because of our cultural lens. Certainly our ability to get in the car, pick up, and drive off like we do and our access to digital cameras allows us to do certain things that some of the nineteenth-century artists, I'm certain, would have loved to used in terms of tools. So that does change our work.

LAURA: The weather dissonance is an example. Pioneers that were at Devil's Gate in a snowstorm miles away from help, rescue, or civilization wouldn't have had the luxury to stop and paint. Part of the ability to capture Devil's Gate in the snow comes from your ability to get in the car and leave. It comes from an approach to do only preparatory studies and finish paintings in your studio. For example, for much of the exhibition, all of the studies were done en plein air, is that correct?

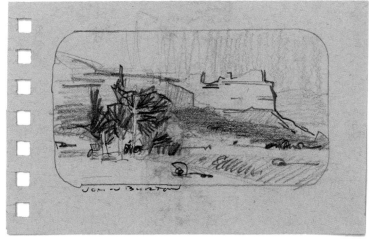

John Burton, Untitled, sketchbook (Scotts Bluff, Nebraska, 2013).

JOHN: Yes. Of course, a landscape painting does not feel the same as being there, but it evokes a poetic, even lyrical, memory of the emotion felt while witnessing it. This is why it was important for us to hike out day after day in all weather conditions with our paints and easels and return with a small sketch or study that we could bring back to our studio and develop into a finished piece. Painting on-site allowed us to bring the sense of the site and embed it into each artwork.

LAURA: How did you go about painting and traveling the trail? And how long have you been working on this project?

JOHN: I believe we started this project in the fall of 2011, when Bryan and I flew to Casper, Wyoming, where we first picked up the trail at Mormon Ferry and made our way to Salt Lake.

JOSH: That's right. We took it in segments—Nauvoo to Casper in 2012, Nauvoo to Omaha in 2014, and a whole bunch of Wyoming and Utah trips in between.

BRYAN: Over a several-year period we would travel a week at a time to different sections of the trail during different times of the year to capture all four seasons. We wanted to have a fuller experience so we could understand better what the Mormon pioneers went through when crossing the trail.

LAURA: Like the pioneers themselves, you compared the trail to Moses's exodus, but that image is really rooted in the land, right?

JOHN: While working on these paintings, I have often wondered what it would be like to have had three artists document Moses's exodus out of Egypt. How incredible it would be to see those paintings, even if, as in our case, they were done 150 to 170 years after the fact. Something of the land would still exist, and in looking at the paintings, the viewer could become a witness of what had transpired there. I am grateful we had the opportunity to walk on this sacred ground. Linking each painting with journal entries and reminiscences helped ground the paintings in the stories of the trail.

Bryan Mark Taylor painting near Garden Grove, Iowa, spring 2015.

LAURA: What about the landscape most appealed to you? Were there any particular areas you found picturesque?

BRYAN: The big open skies, grand sweeping vistas, rivers, and prominent landmarks are always awe inspiring. However, some of the smaller, more intimate details like wagon ruts, names carved in the stone, and forts and ferries discovered along the way were also very interesting.

JOHN: Truth be told, the main reason it appealed to me was the history. The Mormon pioneers were looking for the safest and flattest route, not the scenic route. It was the love of the project that kept me going on days that I was struggling to find a composition in some of the land, on days when I struggled with the landscape and I couldn't create anything. A few days before our first trip out, Bryan and I started looking at vast areas of the trail using Google Earth, and we almost canceled because we were not sure how we would make interesting paintings out of the flat, nondescript land.

JOSH: For me, the landscape was everything, and the more I looked at the land, the more I fell in love with it. The entire trail is special. Initially I thought we'd taken on a great challenge—to make beautiful paintings out of a landscape that most people think mundane. Yet, it's far from mundane—it's just subtle, and most people don't have time for subtlety. The more I paint, the more I realize that the quiet beauty of ordinary and simple things is the kind of beauty most worth looking for and the most rewarding to find.

LAURA: Exactly. I like this in part because the area is often seen as fly-over territory but also because I think the notion of subtlety is a consistent theme in the show. Was there a specific area you responded to most?

JOHN: I loved Echo Canyon. It had a glory and peacefulness that was unmatched on the trail. If I were a pioneer, I would have wanted to stop right there to build my home.

JOSH: One of the locations that surprised me the most was Mount Pisgah. Not that it was any more beautiful than the rest of the trail, but I was surprised at how hallowed it was. It felt as holy and, to me, as consecrated as a temple.

LAURA: Why was that so for you, Josh? Although it's noted as a camp in pioneer journals, it's not a site referenced often in lay pioneer history. What pioneer story were you responding to?

JOSH: Actually, it wasn't a particular story. It was just the presence of pioneer marks, raw dugouts. It's pasture largely and had this sense of being untouched. Much of Mount

Pisgah (the mountain, not the city) is just privately owned property.

LAURA: There were relics. Tangible evidence of the Mormon pioneers who had gone before.

JOSH: Yes, and there was something about not having it cleaned up either and not having historic markers or demarcated plaques. It wasn't curated space. There were spots where you could see wagon ruts going across a little stream, and you can see remnants of dugouts, but it's just been sitting there. It felt untouched, just left there. And someone hadn't built a home there or over it. That was part of why it was amazing. But it was also just the land itself. It just felt really sacred.

LAURA: And part of that goes back to your original premise, where you wanted to capture the landscape now because the pioneers are still a part of relatively recent history. In part, because there are areas that still look the same.

JOSH: Mount Pisgah especially. The rest of the trail is really special, but the mark of the pioneers has been erased more in other places.

LAURA: Like Casper, Evanston, Salt Lake, to name a few.

JOSH: Exactly. Near Evanston, we had a guide who showed us around and pointed out little dips in the ground, evidence of wagon trains. And that was special for us. Because, even with maps, there are some areas where we felt like we were only generally in the right area, and in that sense, there is an element of guesswork.

LAURA: What specific pioneer story did you most respond to? Did you do research on individual companies or Mormon pioneers as you prepared your trips and mapped out your location?

JOHN: For me, it was Robert Taylor Burton, my ancestor. On February 11, 1846, as refugees, he and his family and new bride crossed a bitterly cold Mississippi River. His young wife would refer to their five-month cold and soggy crossing of Iowa as their "wedding tour." In his journal, Robert reported that his wife was so sick with fever she would shake the covered wagon with her chills.

His sixty-year-old mother, who greatly suffered from exposure after being chased from her comfortable Illinois home, passed away while fleeing. Later on the trail, they were stranded after their oxen team drank alkali water and died.

However, he would later retrace that trail several times. He braved very deep snow and harsh conditions to rescue the Willie and Martin handcart companies. Robert's oldest son, William, wrote, "Father could seldom be induced to talk of this trip, saying it was too sad and heartrending to even recall to memory, let alone tell it." Robert later in 1907 wrote about the rescue, "In spite all that we could do many were laid to rest by the wayside. These matters I do not desire to dwell upon. I would rather forget them and look [at] the brighter side, and thank the Lord for his kind providence in saving those whom he did spare."[2]

I most responded to Robert Taylor Burton's incredible experience as a pioneer because in our "me" generation, he sets an example of sacrificing for his beliefs and serving others.

Though my parents were not Latter-day Saints, they often shared stories of Robert Burton and my other ancestors who braved the trail. I was grateful for their journals and other accounts of their lives, and through these stories, I was compelled by their extraordinary sacrifice and commitment to faith. The more I learned about them, the more I wanted to understand their faith through reading the scriptures. As I read the Book of Mormon and prayed, I received a testimony. For me, Mormon pioneers have been an incredible role model of how, with faith, we can not only persevere through trials but how our trials can propel us to accomplish great things.

JOSH: In one of the books I read, I made notes in the margin to dedicate a painting to Hosea Stout and to dedicate another to Margaret and Samuel Pucell. Two stories of many, but they touched me deeply.

LAURA: To dedicate a painting to a specific pioneer is a big gesture. Are they relatives? Why did you identify so closely with them, and why did they evoke such a sense of dedication? Can you talk about one specifically?

JOSH: I read about Hosea Stout in the book *The Gathering*. It includes an account from his journal where he writes:

[I] found the poor little afflicted child in the last agonies of death. He died in my arms about 4 o'clock.... I shall not attempt to say anything about my feelings at this time.... My wife is yet unable to go about, and little Hosea my only son now is wearing down with the same complaint, and what will be the end thereof? We are truly desolate and afflicted, and entirely destitute of anything even to eat, much less to nourish the sick, and just able to go about myself. Arrangements made to bury him this evening.[3]

Mormon pioneer Hosea Stout was thirty-five years old during the exodus across Iowa.

Hosea lost his wife and all of his children on this journey. On January 7, 2016, I scribbled a note to myself in the margin of *The Gathering* about dedicating a painting to him, and on January 18, my youngest daughter, Emily, was born. I now have three children of my own, and watching them suffer and having no way to relieve that suffering would be worse than death for me. I think that's why this particular story resonated deeply with me. They are stories of parents like me, parents who worshipped the God I worship and who trusted him enough to give him their all—holding nothing back. Not all the Saints who crossed the plains were asked to physically give everything the way these two families were, but as Christ told the Nephites in the Book of Mormon, the sacrifice the Lord requires of all of us is that of a broken heart and a contrite spirit (see 3 Nephi 9:20). We—all of us—must be "willing to observe [our] covenants by sacrifice" (Doctrine and Covenants 97:8).

Heavenly Father, through the grace of his Son, Jesus Christ, helped Hosea offer that sacrifice, and I know he can help me to do the same. Their examples inspire and encourage me—they make me want to try harder and be better.

LAURA: Certainly having a child while reading that account would make it all the more personal, and I think you would get a real sense of the depth of Stout's vulnerability, loss, rawness, and sacrifice. We've touched on this point a bit, but what links you and your life today to these landscapes and the stories of the pioneers?

JOSH: Consecration. The pioneers gave everything they had to follow God, to put him first, and we can do that too. Our sacrifices are admittedly different, but they work the same change on our hearts. We can give God our whole hearts just as surely as they gave theirs, and he expects us to do so. That's why we're here. I've got a long way to go, but my prayer is that this show will be both a start for myself and others and a chance to remember and recommit.

BRYAN: I agree. On the way over, I was listening to National Public Radio and thinking about a number of issues going on in the world today and how this project relates to, and is maybe a response to, that suffering—a kind of healing balm in a way. There are a lot of politically divisive things going on today, not just in the United States, but all around the world—the Syrian refugee crisis, or by contrast, the political rhetoric of nationalism and "othering" of immigrants and religious groups, the rampant xenophobia, or at the very least the tumultuous tension between Islam and Christianity happening in many countries.

LAURA: Yes. The Mormon Trail wasn't forged out of mere curiosity or desire for a great adventure (though that was part of the experience to some extent; adventure was a byproduct of it), but rather it started as a desperate need to escape persecution. They were refugees. They were strange. They were other.

BRYAN: Right. I guess when I look at a project like this, my hope is one of compassion. You know, to a certain degree, we all, or at least many people, have wandered, have been oppressed, have looked for a home, have looked for acceptance. I'm not trying to be on one side or the other in these political movements. My hope is that we can better understand different groups and the things they went through and have more compassion for people who do not think like us. I guess, in a sense, that's really what I'm talking about. Art is a great way to do it because it can be nonconfrontational and it speaks, to some degree, of a universal language and allows you to see the beauty of different cultures. Where I think or feel differently from various people across the world, I can appreciate their culture and the beautiful things they have created. In that spirit, I hope this project can help build a better understanding.

LAURA: Part of the Mormon pioneer story and the paintings you made as tribute to that story are about witnessing human suffering, what it means to be a refugee, what it means to be marginalized within a community, and what it means to be other. And those issues are complex and, at times, fraught.

But there is something really nice about looking at this message on a micro level: it's not about the Mormon problem in the nineteenth century, which can now be used as a metaphor for twenty-first-century refugee problems, but it's about the *one* refugee boy whose boat washes up on shore. It's about the *one* Mormon pioneer who lost his or her children at a specific geographic spot. It's about the singular stories that then end up having universal application because you imagine as a parent what it could feel like to lose a child or what it feels like as a human to suffer, to wander, and to feel like you don't have a home. I think you do well to tie it to those issues because the pioneer experience remains current. Similar conflicts are still playing out and are not all resolved.

JOSH: Elder Patrick Kearon's talk "Rufuge from the Storm" is a great example. He talked about how we, of all people, should be compassionate because of our own heritage. He said, "As members of the Church, as a people, we don't have to look back far in our history to reflect on times when we were refugees, violently driven from homes and farms over and over again."[4]

John Burton, *Nauvoo,* paint study (Nauvoo, Illinois, 2014).

LAURA: That's right. Sister Linda Burton has also talked about our need to help refugees and displaced people.[5] I think there is this image in our mind's eye of this noble pioneer, and there are a lot of monumental sculptures and paintings that depict these heroic pioneers who stood fearless and tall in the face of great suffering. But the language of identifying them as refugees shifts that image. I don't think it shifts the nobility. But it does shift the image in terms of their vulnerability.

BRYAN: Yes, exactly, and in that sense, it's a world problem. It is not just our ancestors who were brave, who suffered, who were persecuted. At some point, every culture has had to deal with it. And I think it taps into that universal human desire to have a home and an identity.

LAURA: And be accepted. To be loved as the Savior loved.

BRYAN: Right. And I think that before casting a stone, we, as Mormons, should step back and say, "Hey, you know what? My ancestors and, at any point, some part of the human family, have been dealing with being disenfranchised or marginalized." I think this is a way to look back and honor that struggle; you also have to expand that concept not only to how it applies to you personally but how it applies to other groups. Because it's not just our culture that has experienced this struggle. It's every culture. It's a very fundamental story of human struggle.

LAURA: Going back to the title, the moment of *Saints at Devil's Gate* is a human experience. Every person that lives on earth has big trials to face, and those are varied and individual and sometimes even culturally nuanced, but the fact is that the human experience is full of struggle and toil, even amongst profound beauty.

BRYAN: Right. That's the beauty of the concept of *Saints at Devil's Gate*. It's a notion of perseverance. The pioneers, today and yesterday, who, in spite of great challenges and great difficulties, did noble, beautiful things. They helped others. They sacrificed their own lives, and even in times of great personal struggle and personal loss, they rose. They kept walking.

LAURA: It again goes back to that idea of nobility in vulnerability, that they were brave in abject circumstances. And we're called to be brave as well. We're asked be faithful amid uncertainty, and that absolutely requires a type of bravery.

JOSH: Yes. Their bravery was manifested in just continuing, in simply keeping on. Certainly, when you read their journals, you know they weren't superhuman. The Mormon pioneers were scared and angry and bewildered at the losses and at the trials. But the concept of *Saints at Devil's Gate* as a metaphor is so beautiful because "a saint is a sinner who keeps on trying,"[6] and Devil's Gate is the hard stuff that we go through in our lives. We look back and we call it heroism and bravery when, really, I think it was a struggle, like it is for us today. Faith is sometimes one step, just one step, in front of another.

LAURA: Messy, imperfect humans whose faith allows them to keep walking.

JOSH: But it becomes more and more beautiful and mythical as time passes. I think for the Mormon pioneers, it was really rough stuff. If we could get into their minds (and journals help with that) as they held their dying children and just watched, it wouldn't just be perfect faith. There would be a lot of questions, a lot of asking why, and a lot of hopelessness, desperation, and struggle. But they had enough faith to keep on going, even if it was just barely, like barely trusting enough to muscle through the next river.

But that's enough, even to just move forward, just a little bit—that is all God expects.

BRYAN: I think it's very timely in a way. The trail represents a journey we all have to make through life. The way in which we think, act, and experience the trail today is very different from the early Saints. The way in which we view and interpret the landscape today reflects those differences. Yet, among those differences, it has been interesting to discover some universals. These universals give us an access point where we can analyze these similarities and differences, which will help us make a deeper connection to our heritage and to those around us who suffer and whose faith leads them to keep walking.

Within each section of these notes, sources are cited in full on first mention. The following abbreviations are used for certain frequently cited repositories:

BYU L. Tom Perry Special Collections, Harold B. Lee Library, Brigham Young University, Provo, Utah

CHL Church History Library, The Church of Jesus Christ of Latter-day Saints, Salt Lake City

DUP Pioneer Memorial Museum, International Society Daughters of Utah Pioneers, Salt Lake City

Notes to Laura Allred Hurtado, "'More Wonderful Than Beautiful': Painting the Land along the Mormon Trail," pages 1–9

1. The approximately 265-mile segment of the Mormon Trail from Nauvoo to Council Bluffs, Iowa, was used infrequently after the 1846 exodus of Saints from Nauvoo. However, marking the Mormon pioneer journey from Nauvoo to the Salt Lake Valley captured, for the artists, the essence of leaving behind one homeland and journeying to another. (Stanley B. Kimball, "Mormon Pioneer Trail," in *Encyclopedia of Mormonism,* ed. Daniel H. Ludlow, 5 vols. [New York: Macmillan, 1992], 2:943.)

2. Josh Clare, email to the author, Nov. 15, 2013. Describing the project, Clare wrote, "Why we're crazy excited about it: IT FEELS RIGHT! We are SUPER excited to use the talents God has given us not just to try and create beautiful pictures … but beautiful pictures that mean something to us. We've been out twice so far, once in the fall and once this last February for a week. We drove the trail, stopping every couple of minutes to do a very small color sketch and take a billion pictures. The experience was really powerful for all of us. So many sites along the trail have remained untouched—sacred. It's a small way to pay homage to men and women to whom we owe everything, but working on this project has felt incredibly right…. All three of us have felt God's hand in our work and felt His approval of it."

3. James Linforth, ed., *Route from Liverpool to Great Salt Lake Valley: Illustrated with Steel Engravings and Wood Cuts from Sketches Made by Frederick Piercy…* (Liverpool: Franklin D. Richards; London: Latter-day Saints' Book Depot, 1855), vii.

4. Linforth, *Route from Liverpool to Great Salt Lake Valley,* 72.

5. For more information about the Mormon Trail, see "Mormon Pioneer National Historic Trail: IL, IA, NE, UT, WY," United States Department of the Interior, National Park Service, accessed Aug. 30, 2016, http://nps.gov/mopi/index.htm.

6. Of this subjectivity Lucy Lippard said, "They map only what the authors or their employers want to show; resistance is difficult." (Lucy R. Lippard, *The Lure of the Local: Senses of Place in a Multi-*

centered Society [New York: New Press, 1997], 78.) Further, Wallace Stegner in *The Gathering of Zion* references the disaster of the Willie and Martin handcart companies as partly influenced by Piercy's idealization. He writes, "Brother Brigham urged it, his missionaries and agents urged it, Piercy's *Route from Liverpool* showed them idealized scenes of a road along which he and a company of people like themselves had passed without incident." (Wallace Stegner, *The Gathering of Zion: The Story of the Mormon Trail* [New York: McGraw-Hill, 1964], 225.)

7. David Morgan, *The Sacred Gaze: Religious Visual Culture in Theory and Practice* (Berkeley: University of California Press, 2005), 3.

8. William G. Hartley, "The Pioneer Trek: Nauvoo to Winter Quarters," *Ensign,* June 1997, 32–34; William G. Hartley, "Mormons and Early Iowa History (1838 to 1858): Eight Distinct Connections," *Annals of Iowa* 59, no. 3 (Summer 2000): 232–233.

9. Hartley, "Mormons and Early Iowa History," 232–233.

10. See Salman Rushdie, *Imaginary Homelands: Essays and Criticism, 1981–1991* (London: Granta Books, 1992), 10. Referencing his expatriation from India, Rushdie said, "It may be that writers in my position, exiles or emigrants or expatriates, are haunted by some sense of loss, some urge to reclaim, to look back, even at the risk of being mutated into pillars of salt. But if we do look back, we must also do so in the knowledge—which gives rise to profound uncertainties—that our physical alienation from India almost inevitably means that we will not be capable of reclaiming precisely the thing that was lost; that we will, in short, create fictions, not actual cities or villages, but invisible ones, imaginary homelands, Indias of the mind."

11. Ayres Natural Bridge was not given that name until late in the nineteenth century. However, the pioneers would have known the stone formation by sight. See page 66 for Hosea Stout's description.

12. Mormons were not alone as travelers. Along with tens of thousands of Mormon pioneers, other immigrants, including fur trappers, missionaries, soldiers, settlers, miners, freighters, and cattle companies traveled the trail. As rugged as the trail was for these migrants, it was the modern-day highway of its time. What made the Mormon pioneers distinct, of course, was the intent of their migration.

13. In most areas, the Mormon Trail is less curated than Gettysburg National Military Park. Much of it can still be stumbled upon and appears as it was 170 years ago. However, such comparisons are still worthwhile because it is a pilgrimage landscape that has come to signify much more than what appears.

14. In large part, most of the journal excerpts included in the exhibition came from museum research headed by historian Bryon C. Andreasen after the object list was finalized and the work of the artists was completed. However, there were some stories that accompanied the painters as they worked.

15. See Hosea Stout, Reminiscences and Journals, 1845–1869, microfilm, MS 8332, CHL, May 8, June 28, and Sept. 26, 1846.

16. Bryan Mark Taylor, phone call with the author, July 19, 2016.

17. See "Robert Taylor Burton," "Noah Brimhall," and "John Watkins," Mormon Pioneer Overland Travel, 1847–1868, compiled by The Church of Jesus Christ of Latter day Saints, accessed Sept. 7, 2016, http://history.lds.org/overlandtravel.

18. In an interesting convergence, one of my ancestors also participated in the rescue of the Willie and Martin handcart companies. Redick Allred headed up a supply camp that ultimately provided much-needed assistance, including four wagons, to the Willie company. (See "Redick Newton Allred," Mormon Pioneer Overland Travel, accessed Sept. 7, 2016.)

19. Wallace Stegner, "Ordeal by Handcart," *Collier's Magazine,* July 6, 1956, 85.

20. Miwon Kwon, *One Place after Another: Site-Specific Art and Locational Identity* (Cambridge, MA: MIT Press, 2002), 8.

21. Josh Clare, email to the author, June 13, 2016.

22. "About Us," *Outdoor Painter: The Home of PleinAir Magazine,* accessed Sept. 7, 2016, http://www.outdoorpainter.com/about-us.

23. Josh Clare, email to the author, June 15, 2016.

24. Linforth, *Route from Liverpool to Great Salt Lake Valley,* 91.

25. Louisa Barnes Pratt, Journal and Autobiography, 1850–1800, MS 8227, CHL, 146.

26. Samuel Openshaw, Diary, May–Nov. 1856, typescript, MS 1515, CHL, Sept. 16, 1856.

27. William Gilpin, *Three Essays: On Picturesque Beauty; On Picturesque Travel; and On Sketching Landscape: To Which Is Added a Poem, on Landscape Painting* (London: R. Blamire, in the Strand, 1792), 3.

28. "Picturesque," *Oxford English Dictionary,* compiled by Oxford University Press, accessed June 1, 2016, http://www.oed.com.

29. Edmund Burke, *A Philosophical Enquiry into the Origin of Our Ideas of the Sublime and Beautiful and Other Pre-revolutionary Writings,* ed. David Womersley (London: Penguin Books, 1998), 101, italics in original.

30. Burke, *Philosophical Enquiry,* 111.

31. Stegner, "Ordeal by Handcart," 78, 81.

32. Archer Walters, Diary, Mar.–Sept. 1856, typescript, MS 1407, CHL, June 26, 1856.

33. Jean Rio Griffiths Baker, Diary, Jan. 1851–Mar. 1852, Sept. 1869–May 1880, typescript, MS 1788, CHL, Aug. 29, 1851.

34. Sarah Maria Mousley (Cannon), Journal, May–Sept. 1857, MS 23833, CHL, Aug. 25, 1857.

35. Hannah Tapfield King, Autobiography, ca. 1864–1872, MS 1573, CHL, vol. 6, Aug. 28, 1853.

36. Quoted in Kathryn Calley Galitz, "Romanticism," Oct. 2004, Heilbrunn Timeline of Art History, compiled by the Metropolitan Museum of Art, New York City, accessed Sept. 7, 2016, http://www.metmuseum.org/toah/hd/roma/hd_roma.htm.

37. Philip Shaw, *The Sublime* (Oxford: Routledge, 2006), 1–2.

38. David E. Nye, *American Technological Sublime* (Cambridge, MA: MIT Press, 1994), 4. Nye says, "Discussions of the sublime usually begin with Longinus and then jump to early-eighteenth-century England, where the topic was taken up and elaborated by many authors—most notably Edmund Burke, whose *Philosophical Enquiry into the Origin of Our Ideas of the Sublime and Beautiful,* published in 1756, became the most influential work on the subject."

39. Burke, *Philosophical Enquiry,* 111, italics in original.

40. See Moses 1:8, 10.

41. Marjorie Hope Nicolson, *Mountain Gloom and Mountain Glory: The Development of the Aesthetics of the Infinite* (Ithaca, NY: Cornell University Press, 1959), 321–323, as quoted in Nye, *American Technological Sublime,* 2.

42. Doctrine and Covenants 38:18.

Notes to Bryon C. Andreasen, "'Oh How I Wish Mine Were a Painter's Pencil or Poet's Pen': Pioneer Reflections on the Landscape of the Mormon Trail," pages 11–13

1. Stanley B. Kimball, *Historic Resource Study: Mormon Pioneer National Historic Trail* ([Washington DC]: United States Department of the Interior, National Park Service, 1991), 4. Also available at http://files.lib.byu.edu/mormonmigration/articles/MormonPioneerNationalHistoricTrail.PDF.

2. Wallace Stegner, *The Gathering of Zion: The Story of the Mormon Trail* (New York: McGraw-Hill, 1964).

3. Daniel Allen and his daughter Mary Anne Allen (Lowry) were members of the Samuel Gully–Orson Spencer company that followed the Mormon Trail to Utah in 1849. A list of company members is in the Mormon Pioneer Overland Travel database at http://history.lds.org/overlandtravel. (See also "Death of Daniel Allen," *Deseret News* [Weekly], Feb. 13, 1892, 266; Daniel Allen Family Papers, undated, MS 12046, CHL; Daniel Allen, Reminiscences, ca. 1865, MS 11453,

CHL; and "Reminiscences of Maryann Allen Lowry Recorded by Her Daughter Clara Bell Lowry Singleton," photocopy of holograph in author's possession.)

4. William G. Hartley, "Planning the Exodus: 1842–1846," in *Mapping Mormonism: An Atlas of Latter-day Saint History,* ed. Brandon S. Plewe (Provo, UT: Brigham Young University Press, 2012), 68–69; Glen M. Leonard, *Nauvoo: A Place of Peace, a People of Promise* (Salt Lake City: Deseret Book; Provo, UT: Brigham Young University Press, 2002), 512–513, 566; Alexander L. Baugh, "John C. Frémont's 1843–44 Western Expedition and Its Influence on Mormon Settlement in Utah," *Utah Historical Quarterly* 83, no. 4 (Fall 2015): 254–269.

5. Kimball, *Historic Resource Study,* 35–36, 43–45; Leonard, *Nauvoo,* 585, 607–616; William G. Hartley, "The Exodus Begins: 1846," in *Mapping Mormonism,* 72–76. According to Kimball, after the primary use of the Iowa segment of the trail in 1846, portions of the trail were used by some Mormon companies leaving from Keokuk, Iowa, in 1853; by seven handcart companies in 1856–1857 that began their journeys at Iowa City, Iowa, and intersected the 1846 trail at Cass County; and by a few other companies that used variants of the 1846 trail as late as 1863. A good account of the 1846 Iowa trek and wintering on the Missouri River is Richard E. Bennett, *Mormons at the Missouri, 1846–1852* (Norman: University of Oklahoma Press, 1987).

6. This was the distance measured by William Clayton during the vanguard company's trek in 1847. The creation of a "roadometer" (odometer) is one of the most celebrated stories in Mormon Trail literature. Clayton, a church clerk, feared the 1847 vanguard company's daily mileage estimates were inaccurate. So he marked a wagon wheel and counted its rotations. By multiplying the circumference of the wheel (14 feet 8 inches) by the number of revolutions, he could determine the distance traveled. But such counting was tedious. Orson Pratt applied his mathematical mind to the problem and designed a screw-shaft-driven system of interlocked wooden-teethed wheel gears attached to a wagon wheel. Carpenter Appleton Milo Harmon built Pratt's device from a wooden feed box and iron scraps, using his pocketknife and a hammer. Thereafter, Clayton's work of recording mileage became easier and more accurate.

The same William Clayton who used the mechanical mile counter also produced one of the finest Mormon Trail journals in existence; wrote the *Latter-day Saints' Emigrants' Guide* (1848), which was used by most Mormon pioneers who came later; and composed the hymn that became the pioneers' anthem—"All Is Well," known today as "Come, Come, Ye Saints." (Kimball, *Historic Resource Study,* 35; William Clayton, Diaries, 1846–1853, MS 1406, CHL, May 8, 12, 14, and 16, 1853; Richard E. Bennett, *We'll Find the Place: The Mormon Exodus, 1846–1848* [Salt Lake City: Deseret Book, 1997], 137–139; James B. Allen, *No Toil nor Labor Fear: The Story of William Clayton* [Provo, UT: Brigham Young University Press, 2002], 199–200, 219, 228–231, 243–245; Guy E. Stringham, "The Pioneer Roadometer," *Utah Historical Quarterly,* vol. 42, no. 3 [Summer 1974]: 258–272.)

7. Sarah Maria Mousley (Cannon), Journal, May–Sept. 1857, MS 23833, CHL, Aug. 5, 1857. Mousley traveled in the Jacob Hofheins company from June 6 to September 21, 1857. ("Sarah Maria Mousley," Mormon Pioneer Overland Travel, 1847–1868, compiled by The Church of Jesus Christ of Latter-day Saints, accessed July 28, 2016, http://history.lds.org/overlandtravel.)

8. Stegner, *Gathering of Zion,* caption to Chimney Rock illustration between pp. 148–149.

9. Caroline Barnes Crosby, Journal, May 10, 1848–Feb. 7, 1853, Caroline Barnes Crosby, Papers, 1848–1882, MS 8151, CHL, Aug. 11, 1848.

Notes to the Exhibition Text, pages 18–120

1. Harriet Decker Hanks, "A Sketch of My Pioneer Life Written for My Dear Grand Daughter Madie E. Hatch," in *Descendants of Ephraim Knowlton Hanks and His Wives,* comp. Golden Leone and Teton Hanks Jackman (Provo, UT: n.p., n.d.), copy at CHL.

2. Hosea Stout, Reminiscences and Journals, 1845–1869, microfilm, MS 8332, CHL, Feb. 9, 1846.

3. Wilford Woodruff, Journal, May 22, 1846, in *Wilford Woodruff's Journal, 1833–1898,* ed. Scott G. Kenney, 9 vols. (Midvale, UT: Signature Books, 1983–1985), 3:49.

4. Newel Knight, Autobiography and Journal, ca. 1846–1847, MS 767, folder 2, items 70–71, CHL, Apr. 24, 1846.

5. John Watkins, Reminiscences, 1856, typescript, Pioneer History Collection, DUP.

6. Hannah Tapfield King, Autobiography, ca. 1864–1872, MS 1573, CHL, vol. 6, May 29, 1853.

7. Louisa Barnes Pratt, Journal and Autobiography, 1850–1880, MS 8227, CHL, 131.

8. Martha (Patty) Bartlett Sessions (Parry), Diaries and Account Book, 1846–1866, 1880, MS 1462, CHL, Mar. 9, 1846.

9. Louisa Barnes Pratt, Journal and Autobiography, 132.

10. Lorenzo Brown, Diary and Autobiography, 1856–1899, MSS 497, BYU, May 23, 1846.

11. Wallace Stegner, *The Gathering of Zion: The Story of the Mormon Trail* (New York: McGraw-Hill, 1964), 1.

12. William Clayton, Diaries, 1846–1853, MS 1406, CHL, Apr. 6 and 15, 1846.

13. Lorenzo Brown, Diary and Autobiography, May 28, 1846.

14. Carol Cornwall Madsen, *Journey to Zion: Voices from the Mormon Trail* (Salt Lake City, Deseret Book, 1997), 29–33; Leland H. Gentry, "The Mormon Way Stations: Garden Grove and Mt. Pisgah," *BYU Studies,* vol. 21, no. 4 (Fall 1981): 445–461; Historian's Office, History of the Church, 1838–ca. 1882, CR 100 102, CHL, vol. 16, p. 80.

15. Wilford Woodruff, Journal, June 30, 1846, in *Wilford Woodruff's Journal,* 3:55.

16. Louisa Barnes Pratt, Journal and Autobiography, 134.

17. Parley P. Pratt, *The Autobiography of Parley Parker Pratt, One of the Twelve Apostles of the Church of Jesus Christ of Latter-day Saints, Embracing His Life, Ministry and Travels, with Extracts, in Prose and Verse, from His Miscellaneous Writings,* ed. Parley P. Pratt Jr. (New York: Russell Brothers, 1874), 381.

18. William Clayton, Diaries, May 26, 1846.

19. Caroline Barnes Crosby, Journal, May 10, 1848–Feb. 7, 1853, Caroline Barnes Crosby, Papers, 1848–1882, MS 8151, CHL, May 28, 1848.

20. Louisa Barnes Pratt, Journal and Autobiography, 138.

21. Hannah Tapfield King, Autobiography, vol. 6, June 12, 1853.

22. Samuel Openshaw, Diary, May–Nov. 1856, typescript, MS 1515, CHL, Aug. 7, 1856.

23. Desla Slade Bennion, "Biography of Amelia Eliza Slade Bennion," n.d., MS 1874 2, CHL, 13.

24. Louisa Barnes Pratt, Journal and Autobiography, 140.

25. "John Lingren Tells His Story," 1893, typescript, Pioneer History Collection, DUP, 4.

26. "Events in the Life of George Washington and Cynthia Stewart Hill, Utah Pioneers of 1847, as Recorded by Their Son, George Richard Hill," Jan. 1878, typescript, MS 8237 item 57b, CHL, 19.

27. William G. Hartley and A. Gary Anderson, *Sacred Places,* ed. LaMar C. Berrett, vol. 5, *Iowa and Nebraska: A Comprehensive Guide to Early LDS Historical Sites* (Salt Lake City: Deseret Book, 2006), 250–254; William Clayton, Diaries, Apr. 16, 1847; Hannah Tapfield King, Autobiography, vol. 6, p. [13].

28. Eulalia Myler Johnson, "Diary of Henry Stokes," typescript, Pioneer History Collection, DUP, 5.

29. "Events in the Life of George Washington and Cynthia Stewart Hill," 19.

30. "Life Story of Mary Pugh [Scott]," typescript, MSS A 2105-1, Utah State Historical Society, Salt Lake City, 4.

31. Samuel Openshaw, Diary, Sept. 16, 1856.

32. Loleta Dixon, "Willie Handcart Company and William James Account," n.d., MS 1029, CHL, [6]–[7].

33. Caroline Barnes Crosby, Journal, Aug. 4 and 10, 1848.

34. Thomas Bullock, Journals, 1843–1849, MS 1385, CHL, June 11, 1847.

35. Sarah Maria Mousley (Cannon), Journal, May–Sept. 1857, MS 23833, CHL, July 24 and Aug. 5, 1857.

36. Hannah Tapfield King, Autobiography, vol. 6, Aug. 3, 1853.

37. Thomas Bullock, Journals, May 12, 1847.

38. Hannah Tapfield King, Autobiography, vol. 6, Aug. 3 and 5, 1853.

39. Sarah P. Rich, Autobiography, 1884–1893, Autobiography and Journal, 1890–1893, MS 1543, CHL, Aug. 1, 1847, 38.

40. Samuel Openshaw, Diary, Oct. 3, 1856.

41. Martha (Patty) Bartlett Sessions (Parry), Diaries and Account Book, July 29, 1847.

42. John Burton, interview with Laura Allred Hurtado, Jan. 27, 2016, Carmel, CA.

43. Lucy R. Lippard, *The Lure of the Local: Senses of Place in a Multi-centered Society* (New York: New Press, 1997), 8, italics in original.

44. Wilford Hill LeCheminant, "'Entitled to Be Called an Artist': Landscape and Portrait Painter Frederick Piercy," *Utah Historical Quarterly* 48, no. 1 (Winter 1980): 50–65; L. Matthew Chatterley, "Frederick Piercy: English Artist on the American Plains," *Mormon Historical Studies,* vol. 4, no. 2 (Fall 2003): 77–96; James Linforth, ed., *Route from Liverpool to Great Salt Lake Valley: Illustrated with Steel Engravings and Wood Cuts from Sketches Made by Frederick Piercy…* (Liverpool: Franklin D. Richards; London: Latter-day Saints' Book Depot, 1855).

45. Wilford Woodruff, Journal, Aug. 14, 1850, in *Wilford Woodruff's Journal,* 3:568.

46. Linforth, *Route from Liverpool to Great Salt Lake Valley,* 91.

47. "The Journal of Noah Brimhall," typescript, MS 14172, CHL, 13.

48. "Story of Louise Graehl," in Kate B. Carter, comp., *Treasures of Pioneer History,* 6 vols. (Salt Lake City: Daughters of Utah Pioneers, 1952–1957), 4:57.

49. Elijah Averett, Autobiography, Averett Family Notebook, ca. 1916–1965, MS 9100, CHL, 14[a].

50. "John Lingren Tells His Story," 5.

51. Hosea Stout, Reminiscences and Journals, July 31, 1848.

52. Eulalia Myler Johnson, "Diary of Henry Stokes," 10.

53. Robert Taylor Burton, Autobiography, n.d., MS 3005, CHL, 8.

54. "Handcart Stories," n.d., typescript, MS 2230, CHL, 31.

55. Norton Jacob, Reminiscence and Journal, May 1844–Jan. 1852, MS 9111, CHL, June 14, 1847.

56. See Stanley B. Kimball, *Historic Resource Study: Mormon Pioneer National Historic Trail* ([Washington DC]: United States Department of the Interior, National Park Service, 1991), 4. Also available at http://files.lib.byu.edu/mormonmigration/articles/MormonPioneer-NationalHistoricTrail.PDF.

57. Richard E. Bennett, *We'll Find the Place: The Mormon Exodus, 1846–1848* (Salt Lake City: Deseret Book, 1997), 183–184; Kimball, *Historic Resource Study*, 57, 90.

58. Lippard, *Lure of the Local,* 8, 20.

59. Thomas Bullock, Journals, June 19, 1847.

60. Norton Jacob, Reminiscence and Journal, June 19, 1847.

61. Mary Elizabeth Rollins Lightner, Diary, May–Sept. 1863, photocopy, MS 750, CHL, Aug. 11, 1863.

62. William Clayton, Diaries, June 19, 1847.

63. Kimball, *Historic Resource Study*, 10. Kimball determined that after the exodus from Nauvoo in 1846, Mormon immigrants traveling to Utah used fourteen different points of departure. After the railroad reached Utah in 1869, immigrants began riding the train the entire way to Zion. (See Kimball, *Historic Resource Study*, 14–15.)

64. Sarah Maria Mousley (Cannon), Journal, Aug. 25, 1857.

65. Rachel Woolley Simmons, Reminiscences and Journals, 1881–1891, MS 2573 1, CHL, [15]–[16].

66. Elizabeth H. Kingsford, Autobiographical Sketch, n.d., MS 11796, CHL, 5.

67. "John Lingren Tells His Story," 5.

68. Lorenzo Brown, Diary and Autobiography, Aug. 11, 1848.

69. Hannah Tapfield King, Autobiography, vol. 6, Aug. 28, 1853.

70. Historian William G. Hartley writes: "In the history of overland trails migration to the American West, handcarts are an anomaly. Of about 350,000 trail emigrants to Oregon and California and 70,000 to Utah, nearly all traveled in wagon companies. In total, only about 3,000 pioneers went west in ten handcart companies during a five-year period, 1856–1860." (William G. Hartley, "The Place of Mormon Handcart Companies in America's Westward Migration Story," *Annals of Iowa*, vol. 65, no. 2 [Spring–Summer 2006]: 101.)

71. Loleta Dixon, "Willie Handcart Company and William James Account," [13]–[14].

72. George Cunningham, Reminiscences, 1876, typescript, MS 7322, CHL, 4–5.

73. Howard Egan, Journals, Apr.–July 1847, Jan.–Sept. 1855, MS 15207, CHL, June 23, 1847.

74. Caroline Barnes Crosby, Journal, Sept. 22, 1848.

75. Marlene Creates, "Artist Statement," in *Zone 6B: Art in the Environment* (Hamilton, ON, Canada: Hamilton Artists, 2003), 32.

76. Lippard, *Lure of the Local,* 33.

77. Sarah Maria Mousley (Cannon), Journal, Aug. 29, 1857.

78. Sarah P. Rich, Autobiography, Sept. 1, 1847, 40–41.

79. Mary Jane Mount Tanner, Reminiscences and Diary, 1872–1884, MS 8272, CHL, 24–25.

80. Desla Slade Bennion, "Biography of Amelia Eliza Slade Bennion," 13.

81. Caroline Barnes Crosby, Journal, Aug. 4, 1848.

82. Jean Rio Griffiths Baker, Diary, Jan. 1851–Mar. 1852, Sept. 1869–May 1880, typescript, MS 1788, CHL, Aug. 29, 1851, 47.

83. Kimball, *Historic Resource Study*, 58.

84. LaMar C. Berrett and A. Gary Anderson, *Sacred Places*, ed. LaMar C. Berrett, vol. 6, *Wyoming and Utah: A Comprehensive Guide to Early LDS Historical Sites along the Mormon Trail* (Salt Lake City: Deseret Book, 2007), 115–116; Bathsheba Bigler Smith, Journal, June–Oct. 1849, photocopy, MS 670, CHL, Oct. 3, 1849.

85. Lorenzo Brown, Diary and Autobiography, Sept. 3, 1848.

86. Hannah Tapfield King, Autobiography, vol. 6, Sept. 8, 1853.

87. Lorenzo Brown, Diary and Autobiography, Sept. 1, 1848.

88. William Clayton, Diaries, June 29, 1847.

89. To me, this same feeling of the artificial infinite is created in

sealing rooms of Latter-day Saint temples, with the dual mirrors that face each other, creating an echo of reflected images that seemingly go on and on into eternity. However, rather than evoking a sense of being lost, this creates a sense of being grounded in a holy union that seals two people together for eternity.

90. Thomas Weiskel, *The Romantic Sublime: Studies in the Structure and Psychology of Transcendence* (Baltimore: Johns Hopkins University Press, 1976), 26, italics in original.

91. Kimball, *Historic Resource Study*, 3, 9.

92. Caroline Barnes Crosby, Journal, Aug. 11, 1848.

93. Jean Rio Griffiths Baker, Diary, Sept. 19, 1851, [52]–[53].

94. Louisa Barnes Pratt, Journal and Autobiography, 146.

95. Hannah Tapfield King, Autobiography, vol. 6, Sept. 10, 1853.

96. Hannah Tapfield King, Autobiography, vol. 6, Sept. 15 and 17, 1853.

97. Eulalia Myler Johnson, "Diary of Henry Stokes," 17.

98. Patience Loader (Rozsa Archer), Reminiscences, ca. 1890, MS 17362, CHL, 189.

99. "The Handcart Pioneers," in Kate B. Carter, *Treasures of Pioneer History,* 5:289–290.

100. Mary Jane Mount Tanner, Reminiscences and Diary, 28.

101. Caroline Barnes Crosby, Journal, Oct. 10, 1848.

102. Rachel Woolley (Simmons), Reminiscences and Journals, [17]–[18].

103. Jean Rio Griffiths Baker, Diary, Sept. 28, 1851, [55]–[56].

104. Mary Jane Mount Tanner, Reminiscences and Diary, 28–29.

105. Kimball, *Historic Resource Study*, 59–61.

106. Bennett, *We'll Find the Place,* 103, 206–210.

107. Kimball, *Historic Resource Study*, 64; Berrett and Anderson, *Sacred Places*, 297–298.

108. Kate B. Carter, comp., *Our Pioneer Heritage,* vol. 6. (Salt Lake City: Daughters of Utah Pioneers, 1962–1963), 59.

109. Ann Agatha Walker Pratt, "Personal Reminiscences," *Woman's Exponent,* Mar. 15, 1893, 21:139.

110. Levi Jackman, Diary, 1847, MSS 79, Overland Trails Diaries, BYU, July 20, 1847.

111. Ann Agatha Walker Pratt, "Personal Reminiscences," 21:139.

112. "Life Story of Mary Pugh [Scott]," 6.

Notes to "Interview with Artists John Burton, Josh Clare, and Bryan Mark Taylor by Laura Allred Hurtado," pages 123–133

1. Danish convert Peter Olsen Hansen, whom Heber C. Kimball adopted into his family before leaving Nauvoo in 1846, kept a journal on Kimball's behalf and made some drawings in the journal while traveling westward. (Stanley B. Kimball, *Heber C. Kimball: Mormon Patriarch and Pioneer* [Urbana: University of Illinois Press, 1981], 135, and captions to sketches between pp. 126–129; Peter Olsen Hansen, Diaries, ca. 1850–1872, vol. 1, MS 7057, CHL, Salt Lake City.)

2. Janet Burton Seegmiller, *Be Kind to the Poor: The Life Story of Robert Taylor Burton* (Cedar City, UT: Robert Taylor Burton Family Organization, 1988), 55–88, 149–164.

3. Maurine Jensen Proctor and Scot Facer Proctor, *The Gathering: Mormon Pioneers on the Trail to Zion* (Salt Lake City: Deseret Book, 1996), 87–89.

4. Patrick Kearon, "Refuge from the Storm," *Ensign,* May 2016, 111.

5. Linda K. Burton, "'I Was a Stranger,'" *Ensign,* May 2016, 13–15.

6. Nelson Mandela, as quoted in Dale G. Renlund, "Latter-day Saints Keep on Trying," *Ensign,* May 2015, 56.

ART TEXTS

Burke, Edmund. *A Philosophical Enquiry into the Origin of Our Ideas of the Sublime and Beautiful and Other Pre-revolutionary Writings.* Edited by David Womersley. London: Penguin Books, 1998.

Givens, Terryl L. *People of Paradox: A History of Mormon Culture.* New York: Oxford University Press, 2007.

Kwon, Miwon. *One Place after Another: Site-Specific Art and Locational Identity.* Cambridge, MA: MIT Press, 2004.

Lippard, Lucy. *The Lure of the Local: Senses of Place in a Multicentered Society.* New York: New Press, 1997.

———. *On the Beaten Track: Tourism, Art, and Place.* New York: New Press, 1999.

Morgan, David. *The Sacred Gaze: Religious Visual Culture in Theory and Practice.* Berkeley: University of California Press, 2005.

Nye, David E. *American Technological Sublime.* Cambridge, MA: MIT Press, 1994.

PleinAir Magazine. West Palm Beach, FL. 2004–2005, 2011–. See also outdoorpainter.com.

Rushdie, Salman. *Imaginary Homelands: Essays and Criticism, 1981–1991.* London: Granta Books, 1992.

Shaw, Philip. *The Sublime.* Oxford: Routledge, 2006.

Stern, Jean, and Molly Siple. *California Light—A Century of Landscapes: Paintings of the California Art Club.* New York: Skira Rizzoli, 2011.

Weiskel, Thomas. *The Romantic Sublime: Studies in the Structure and Psychology of Transcendence.* Baltimore: Johns Hopkins University Press, 1976.

Wolf, Bryan Jay. *Romantic Re-vision: Culture and Consciousness in Nineteenth-Century American Painting and Literature.* Chicago: University of Chicago Press, 1982.

HISTORICAL TEXTS

Bennett, Richard E. *We'll Find the Place: The Mormon Exodus, 1846–1848.* Salt Lake City: Deseret Book, 1997.

Hafen, LeRoy R., and Ann W. Hafen. *Handcarts to Zion: The Story of a Unique Western Migration, 1856–1860, with Contemporary Journals, Accounts, Reports, and Rosters, of Members of the Ten Handcart Companies.* Glendale, CA: Arthur H. Clark, 1960.

Kimball, Stanley B. *Historic Resource Study: Mormon Pioneer National Historic Trail.* [Washington DC]: United States Department of the Interior, National Park Service, 1991. Also available at files.lib.byu.edu/mormonmigration/articles/MormonPioneerNationalHistoricTrail.PDF.

———, ed. *The Latter-day Saints' Emigrants' Guide.* Annotated facsimile of William Clayton's original 1848 publication. Gerald, MO: Patrice Press, 1983.

Kimball, Stanley B., and Violet T. Kimball. *Villages on Wheels: A Social History of the Gathering to Zion.* Salt Lake City: Greg Kofford Books, 2011.

Linforth, James, ed. *Route from Liverpool to Great Salt Lake Valley: Illustrated with Steel Engravings and Wood Cuts from Sketches Made by Frederick Piercy....* Liverpool: Franklin D. Richards; London: Latter-day Saints' Book Depot, 1855.

Madsen, Carol Cornwall. *Journey to Zion: Voices from the Mormon Trail.* Salt Lake City: Deseret Book, 1997.

Madsen, Susan Arrington. *I Walked to Zion: True Stories of Young Pioneers on the Mormon Trail.* Salt Lake City: Deseret Book, 1994.

Mormon Pioneer Overland Travel, 1847–1868. Compiled by The Church of Jesus Christ of Latter-day Saints. http://history.lds.org/overlandtravel.

Stegner, Wallace. *The Gathering of Zion: The Story of the Mormon Trail.* New York: McGraw-Hill, 1964.

TRAIL TRAVEL GUIDEBOOKS

Berrett, LaMar C., and A. Gary Anderson. *Sacred Places.* Edited by LaMar C. Berrett. Vol. 6, *Wyoming and Utah: A Comprehensive Guide to Early LDS Historical Sites along the Mormon Trail.* Salt Lake City: Deseret Book, 2007.

Hartley, William G., and A. Gary Anderson. *Sacred Places.* Edited by LaMar C. Berrett. Vol. 5, *Iowa and Nebraska: A Comprehensive Guide to Early LDS Historical Sites.* Salt Lake City: Deseret Book, 2006.

Kimball, Stanley B. *The Mormon Pioneer Trail, MTA 1997 Official Guide.* Salt Lake City: Mormon Trails Association, 1997.

Kimball, Stanley B., and Violet T. Kimball. *Mormon Trail: Voyage of Discovery—The Story behind the Scenery.* [Las Vegas]: KC Publications, 1995.

COFFEE TABLE BOOKS

Holzapfel, Richard Neitzel. *Their Faces toward Zion: Voices and Images of the Trek West.* Salt Lake City: Bookcraft, 1996.

Kipp, Kathy. *Art Journey America Landscapes: 89 Painters' Perspectives.* Cincinnati: North Light Books, 2012.

Nelson, Glen. *The Glen and Marcia Nelson Collection of Mormon Art.* 2nd ed. New York: Mormon Artists Group, 2015. PDF e-book.

Olsen, Andrew D., Jolene S. Allphin, and Julie Rogers. *Follow Me to Zion: Stories from the Willie Handcart Pioneers.* Salt Lake City: Deseret Book, 2013.

Proctor, Maurine Jensen, and Scot Facer Proctor. *The Gathering: Mormon Pioneers on the Trail to Zion.* Salt Lake City: Deseret Book, 1996.

Rosenblum, Robert, and H. W. Janson. *19th-Century Art.* New York: Harry N. Abrams, 1984.

Slaughter, William W., and Michael Landon. *Trail of Hope: The Story of the Mormon Trail.* Salt Lake City: Shadow Mountain, 1997.

Swinton, Heidi S., and Lee Groberg. *Sweetwater Rescue: The Willie and Martin Handcart Story.* Salt Lake City: Covenant Communications, 2006.

ARTISTS

JOHN BURTON

John Burton is an award-winning oil painter best known for his stirring and vivid depictions of the transitory beauty of our ever-changing world. A graduate of Academy of Art University, Burton has traveled and painted around the globe, always maintaining his home in the American West. Burton's deep American roots permeate the rich, natural character of his art and inform his work's reverent tone. John is married with four children.

JOSH CLARE

Josh Clare graduated with a BFA in illustration from BYU-Idaho in 2007 and has earned numerous awards, including Artists' Choice at the 2012 Laguna Plein Air Invitational and second place in the Raymar 6th Annual Art Painting Competition. His work has been featured in *Western Art & Architecture*, *Southwest Art*, and *Art of the West*. He lives with his wife, Cambree, and their children, Nathan, Anna, and Emily, in Cache Valley, Utah.

BRYAN MARK TAYLOR

An avid traveler and an accomplished painter, Bryan Mark Taylor has won numerous top awards at the most prestigious plein air invitationals and is regularly featured in western art magazines. His work can be found in private, corporate, and museum collections around the world. He received his BA from Brigham Young University in 2001 and his MFA from Academy of Art University in 2005. He lives with his wife and four children in Alpine, Utah.

CURATOR

LAURA ALLRED HURTADO

Laura Allred Hurtado works as the global acquisitions art curator for the Church History Museum, The Church of Jesus Christ of Latter-day Saints, Salt Lake City, Utah. She has curated exhibitions at the Utah Museum of Fine Arts, the Utah Museum of Contemporary Art, CUAC Contemporary, Alice Gallery, Rio Gallery, Snow College, and the Granary Art Center. Previously she worked at the San Francisco Museum of Modern Art, the Brigham Young University Museum of Art, and the Utah Museum of Contemporary Art.

HISTORIAN

BRYON C. ANDREASEN

Bryon C. Andreasen earned a JD at Cornell University and a PhD in nineteenth-century American history at the University of Illinois at Urbana-Champaign. He is currently a historian at the Church History Museum, The Church of Jesus Christ of Latter-day Saints, Salt Lake City, Utah. Previously he was the research historian at the Abraham Lincoln Presidential Library and Museum in Springfield, Illinois, where he also edited the *Journal of the Abraham Lincoln Association* and helped found the Looking for Lincoln Heritage Coalition that pioneered heritage tourism in Illinois.